W9-ADA-595

SEMIOTEXT(E) INTERVENTION SERIES

© 2012 by Franco "Bifo" Berardi

All rights reserved. No part of this book may be reproduced, stored in a retrieval system, or transmitted by any means, electronic, mechanical, photocopying, recording, or otherwise, without prior permission of the publisher.

Published by Semiotext(e)
PO Box 629, South Pasadena, CA 91031
www.semiotexte.com

Earlier versions of portions of this book were published in the web-magazine *e-flux* in spring 2011.

Thanks to Robert Dewhurst, John Ebert, Marc Lowenthal and Jason Smith.

Design: Hedi El Kholti

ISBN: 978-1-58435-112-2
Distributed by The MIT Press, Cambridge, Mass.
and London, England
Printed in the United States of America

10 9 8 7 6 5

Franco "Bifo" Berardi

The Uprising

On Poetry and Finance

semiotext(e)
intervention
series □ 14

Contents

Introduction

These texts were written in 2011, the first year of the European uprising, when European society entered into a deep crisis that seems to me much more a crisis of social imagination than mere economics. Economic dogma has taken hold of the public discourse for three decades, and has destroyed the critical power of political reason. The collapse of the global economy has exposed the dangers of economic dogmatism, but its ideology has already been incorporated into the automatisms of living society.

Political decision has been replaced by techno-linguistic automatisms embedded in the inter-connected global machine, and social choices are submitted to psychic automatisms embedded in social discourse and in the social imaginary.

But the depth of the catastrophe represented by the collapse is awakening hidden potencies of the social brain. The financial collapse marks the beginning of an insurrection whose first glimpses were seen in London, Athens, and Rome in December 2010, and which became massive in the May-June *acampada* in Spain, in the four August nights of rage in the English suburbs, and in the wave of strikes and occupations in the US.

The European collapse is not simply the effect of a crisis that is only economic and financial—this is a crisis of imagination about the future, as well. The Maastricht rules have become unquestionable dogmas, algorithmic formulae and magical spells guarded by the high priests of the European Central Bank and promoted by stockbrokers and advisors.

Financial power is based on the exploitation of precarious, cognitive labor: the general intellect in its present form of separation from the body.

The general intellect, in its present configuration, is fragmented and dispossessed of self-perception and self-consciousness. Only the conscious mobilization of the erotic body of the general intellect, only the poetic revitalization of language, will open the way to the emergence of a new form of social autonomy.

Irreversibility

It's difficult for someone of my generation to break free of the intellectual automatism of the dialectical happy ending.

[handwritten margin annotations: economic dogma / upheld by labor / separated from "body" + automatisms ⇒ crisis of social imagination.]

Just as the Vienna Congress's restoration was followed by the People's Spring in 1848, just as fascism was followed by resistance and liberation, so now the political instinct of my generation (the '68 generation, the last modern generation, in a sense) is expecting the restoration of democracy, the return of social solidarity, and the reversal of financial dictatorship.

This expectation may be deceptive, and we should be able to enhance the space of our historical prefiguration, so as to become able to abandon the conceptual framework of historical progress, and to imagine the prospect of irreversibility. In the sphere of the current bio-economic totalitarianism, the incorporation of techno-linguistic automatisms produced by semio-capital has produced a form that is not an external domination that acts on the body, but a mutation of the social organism itself. This is why historical dialectics no longer work at the level of understanding the process and the prospects: the prospect of irreversibility is replacing the prospect of subversion, so we have to rethink the concept of autonomy from this perspective.

"Irreversibility" is a taboo word in modern political discourse, because it contradicts the principle of rational government of the flow of events—which is the necessary condition of rational government, and the primary contribution of humanism to the theory and the practice of modern politics. Machiavelli speaks of the Prince as a male force who is able to subdue *fortuna* (chance, the chaotic flow of events), the female side of history.

What we are experiencing now, in the age of infinite acceleration of the infosphere, is the following: feminine *fortuna* can no longer be subjected and domesticated by the masculine force of political reason, because *fortuna* is embodied in the chaotic flows of the overcrowded infosphere and in the chaotic flows of financial microtrading. The disproportion between the arrival rate of new information and the limited time available for conscious processing generates hypercomplexity. Therefore projects that propose to rationally change the whole social field are out of the picture.

The horizon of our time is marked by the Fukushima event. Compared to the noisy catastrophes of the earthquake and the tsunami, Tokyo's silent apocalypse is more frightening and suggests a new framework of social expectation for daily life on the planet. The megalopolis is directly exposed to the Fukushima fallout, but life is proceeding almost normally. Only a few people have abandoned the city. Most citizens have stayed there, buying mineral water as they have always done, breathing with face masks on their mouths as they have always done. A few cases of air and water contamination are denounced. Concerns about food safety have prompted US officials to halt the importation of certain foods from Japan. But the Fukushima effect does not imply a disruption of social life: poison has become a normal feature of daily life, the second nature we have to inhabit.

During the last few years disruptions have multiplied in the planetary landscape, but they have not produced a change in the dominant paradigm, a conscious movement of self-organization, or a revolutionary upheaval.

The oil spill in the Gulf of Mexico has not led to the eviction of BP, it has rather consolidated its power, because BP was the only force which could manage the disruption and hopefully bring it under control.

The financial collapse of September 2008 did not lead to a change in US economic politics. Despite the hopes raised by Barack Obama's victory, the financial class did not relax its grip on the economy.

In Europe, after the Greek crisis in 2010, neoliberal ideology—although clearly the source of the collapse—has not been dismissed. On the contrary, the Greek disruption (and the following Irish and Italian and Spanish and Portuguese disruptions) has strengthened the rigor of monetarist policies and stressed the prospect of reducing salaries and social spending.

At a systemic level, change is taking the form of positive feedback.

In his work on cybernetics, Norbert Wiener speaks of negative feedback in order to define the output of a system when it acts to oppose changes to the input of the system, with the result that the changes are reduced and attenuated. If the overall feedback of the system is negative, then the system will tend to be stable. In the social field, for instance, we can say that the system is exhibiting negative feedback if protests and fights oblige the industry to increase salaries and reduce exploitation when social misery becomes too hard and too widespread.

In Wiener's parlance, a system exhibits positive feedback when, on the contrary, it increases the magnitude of a perturbation in response to the perturbation itself. Obviously, unintended positive feedback may be far from being "positive" in the sense of desirable. We can also speak of self-reinforcing feedback.

My impression is this: in conditions of info-acceleration and hypercomplexity, as the conscious and rational will becomes unable to check and to adjust the trends, the trends themselves become self-reinforcing up to the point of final collapse. Look at the vicious circle: right-wing electoral victories and dictatorships of ignorance. When right-wing parties win, their first preoccupation is to impoverish public schooling and to prop up media conformism. The result of the spread of ignorance and conformism will be a new electoral victory, and so on. This is why it is difficult not to see the future of Europe as a dark blend of techno-financial authoritarianism and aggressive populist reaction.

Autonomy, in this condition, will be essentially the ability to escape environments where the positive feedback is switched on. How is it possible to do that, when we know that the planetary environment and global society are increasingly subjected to this catastrophic trend?

How can we think of a process of subjectivation when precarity is jeopardizing social solidarity and when the social body is wired by techno-linguistic automatisms which reduce its activity to a repetition of embedded patterns of behavior?

With this book, I am trying to develop the theoretical suggestions of Christian Marazzi, Paolo Virno, and Maurizio Lazzarato in an unusual direction. These thinkers have conceptualized the relation between language and the economy, and described the subsumption and the subjugation of the biopolitical sphere of affection and language to financial capitalism. I am looking for a way to subvert this subjugation, and I try to do that from the unusual perspectives of poetry and sensibility.

Swarm

When the social body is wired by techno-linguistic automatisms, it acts as a swarm: a collective organism whose behavior is automatically directed by connective interfaces.

A multitude is a plurality of conscious and sensitive beings sharing no common intentionality, and showing no common pattern of behavior. The crowd shuffling in the city moves in countless different directions with countless different motivations. Everybody goes their own way, and the intersection of those displacements makes a crowd. Sometimes the crowd moves in a coordinated way: people run together towards the station because the train is soon expected to leave, people stop together at traffic lights. Everybody moves following his or her will, within the constraints of social interdependency.

If we want to understand something more about the present social subjectivity, the concept of the multitude needs to be complemented with the concepts of the network and swarm.

A network is a plurality of organic and artificial beings, of humans and machines who perform common actions thanks to procedures that make possible their interconnection and interoperation. If you do not adapt to these procedures, if you don't follow the technical rules of the game, you are not playing the game. If you don't react to certain stimuli in the programmed way, you don't form part of the network. The behavior of persons in a network is not aleatory, like the movements of a crowd, because the network implies and predisposes pathways for the networker.

A swarm is a plurality of living beings whose behavior follows (or seems to follow) rules embedded in their neural systems. Biologists call a swarm a multitude of animals of similar size and bodily orientation, moving together in the same direction and performing actions in a coordinated way, like bees building a hive or moving toward a plant where they can find resources for making honey.

In conditions of social hypercomplexity, human beings tend to act as a swarm. When the infosphere is too dense and too fast for a conscious elaboration of information, people tend to conform to shared behavior. In a letter to John Seabrook, Bill Gates wrote: "the digital revolution is all about facilitation—creating tools to make things easy" (Seabrook, 52). In a broader sense, we may say that in the digital age, power is all about making things easy.

In a hypercomplex environment that cannot be properly understood and governed by the individual mind, people will follow simplified pathways and will use complexity-reducing interfaces.

This is why social behavior today seems to be trapped into regular and inescapable patterns of interaction. Techno-linguistic procedures, financial obligations, social needs, and psycho-media invasion—all this capillaric machinery is framing the field of the possible, and incorporating common cognitive patterns in the behavior of social actors.

So we may say that social life in the semiocapital sphere is becoming a swarm.

In a swarm it is not impossible to say "no." It's irrelevant. You can express your refusal, your rebellion and your nonalignment, but this is not going to change the direction of the swarm, nor is it going to affect the way in which the swarm's brain is elaborating information.

Automation of Language

The implication of language in the financial economy is crucial in the contemporary process of subjectivation.

In this book, I am trying to think about the process of emancipating language and affects, and I start from the concept of insolvency.

Insolvency is not only a refusal to pay the costs of the economic crisis provoked by the financial class, but it is also a rejection of the symbolic debt embodied in the cultural and psychic normalization of daily life. Misery is based on the cultural conformism of the nuclear family, on the secluded privacy of individual existence. Privatization of needs and affects has subjected social energies to the chain of capitalist culture. The history of capitalist domination cannot be dissociated from the production and privatization of need—i.e., the creation of cultural and psychic habits of dependence. Social insolvency means independence from the list of priorities that capitalist conformism has imposed on society.

From a linguistic and affective point of view, insolvency is the line of escape from the reduction of language to exchange.

The connective sign recombines automatically in the universal language machine: the digital-financial machine that codifies existential flows. The word is drawn into this process of automation, so we find it frozen and abstract in the disempathetic life of a society that has become incapable of solidarity and autonomy. The automation of the word takes place on two levels.

The first level concerns monetarization and subjection to the financial cycle: signs fall under the domination of finance when the financial function (the accumulation of value through semiotic circulation) cancels the instinctual side of enunciation, so that what is enunciated may be compatible with digital-financial formats. The production of meaning and of value takes the form of parthenogenesis: signs produce signs without any longer passing through the flesh.

financial cycle.

Monetary value produces more monetary value without being first realized through the material production of goods.

A second level is indexicalization. In his paper titled "Quand les mots valent de l'or," Frédéric Kaplan speaks of the process of language's indexicalization in the framework of Internet search engines. Two algorithms define the reduction of linguistic meaning to economic value via a Google search: the first finds the various occurrences of a word, the second links words with monetary value.

The subsumption of language by the semio-capitalist cycle of production effectively freezes the affective potencies of language.

The history of this subsumption passes through the twentieth century, and poetry predicted and prefigured the separation of language from the affective sphere. Ever since Rimbaud called for a *dérèglement de tous les sens*, poets have experimented with the forgetting of the referent and with the autonomous evocation of the signifier.

The experience of French and Russian symbolism broke the referential-denotative link between the word and the world. At the same time, symbolist poets enhanced the connotational potency of language to the point of explosion and hyperinclusion. Words became polysemous evocations for other words, and thus became epiphanic. This magic of postreferential language anticipated the general process of dereferentialization that occurred when the economy became a semio-economy.

The financialization of the capitalist economy implies a growing abstraction of work from its useful function, and of communication from its bodily dimension. As symbolism experimented with the separation of the linguistic signifier from its denotational and referential function, so financial capitalism, after internalizing linguistic potencies, has separated the monetary signifier from its function of denotation and reference to physical goods. Financial signs have led to a parthenogenesis of value, creating money through money without the generative intervention of physical matter and muscular work. Financial parthenogenesis sucks down and dries up every social and linguistic potency, dissolving the products of human activity, especially of collective semiotic activity.

The word is no longer a factor in the conjunction of talking affective bodies, but a connector of signifying functions transcodified by the economy. Once deprived of its conjunctive ability, the word becomes a recombinant function, a discreet (versus continuous) and formalized (versus instinctual) operator.

In 1977 the American anthropologist Rose Khon Goldsen, in *The Show and Tell Machine*, wrote the following words: "We are breeding a new generation of human beings who will learn more words from a machine than from their mothers."

That generation is here. The connective generation entering the social scene today fully suffers the pathogenic and disempathetic effects of the automation of the word.

Poetry and the Deautomation of Language

We have too many things and not enough forms.
—Gustave Flaubert, *Préface à la vie d'écrivain*

Form fascinates when one no longer has the force to understand force from within itself.
—Jacques Derrida, *Writing and Difference*

The voice and poetry are two strategies for reactivation. Once poetry foresaw the abandonment of referentiality and the automation of language; now poetry may start the process of reactivating the emotional body, and therefore of reactivating social solidarity, starting from the reactivation of the desiring force of enunciation.

For Giorgio Agamben, in *Language and Death*, the voice is the point of conjunction between meaning and flesh. The voice is the bodily singularity of the signifying process, and cannot be reduced to the operational function of language, notwithstanding the research in protocols and procedures for vocal recognition.

Poetry is the voice of language, in this sense: it is the reemergence of the deictic function (from *deixis*, self-indication) of enunciation. Poetry is the here and now of the voice, of the body, and of the word, sensously giving birth to meaning.

While the functionality of the operational word implies a reduction of the act of enunciation to connective recombinability, poetry is the excess of sensuousness exploding into the circuitry of social communication and opening again the dynamic of the infinite game of interpretation: desire.

In the introdution to the first volume of his seminal book *Du Sens*, Algirdas Julien Greimas speaks of interpretation as an infinite slippage of the transition from signifier to signified.

This infinite slippage (or slide, or drift) is based on the intimate ambiguity of the emotional side of language (language as excess movement).

We have to start a process of deautomating the word, and a process of reactivating sensuousness (singularity of enunciation, the voice) in the sphere of social communication.

Desire is monstruous, it is cruel, and noncompliance and nonrecombinability are at the inmost nature of singularity. Singularity cannot be compliant with a finite order of interpretation, but it can be compassionate with the infinite ambiguity of meaning as sensuous understanding.

is sensibility open to the perception of uncountable sensuous beings, the condition for an autonomous becoming-other, beyond the financial freeze, beyond the techno-linguistic conformism that is making social life a desert of meaning.

Poetic language is the insolvency in the field of enunciation: it refuses the exaction of a semiotic debt. Deixis (δεῖξις) acts against the reduction of language to indexicalization and abstract individuation, and the voice acts against the recombinant desensualization of language.

poetry

Poetic language is the occupation of the space of communication by words which escape the order of exchangeability: the road of excess, says William Blake, leads to the palace of wisdom. And wisdom is the space of singularity, bodily signification, the creation of sensuous meaning.

the poetic excess.

vs

hypercomplexity (fortuna)

⇒ two "female" forces?

1

THE EUROPEAN COLLAPSE

THE FINANCIAL BLACK HOLE AND THE VANISHING WORLD

alienation of labor.

Finance is the most abstract level of economic symbolization. It is the culmination of a process of progressive abstraction that started with capitalist industrialization. Marx speaks of abstract labor in the sense of an increased distancing of human activity from its concrete usefulness. In his words, capitalism is the application of human skills as a means to obtain a more abstract goal: the accumulation of value. Nevertheless, in the age of industrialization analyzed by Marx, the production *mediation of material* useful goods was still a necessary step in the process of valorization itself. In order to produce abstract value, the industrial capitalist was obliged to produce useful things. This is no longer the case today, in the sphere of semio-capital. In the world of financial capitalism, accumulation no longer passes through the production of goods, but goes straight to its monetary goal, extracting value from the pure circulation of money, from the virtualization of life and intelligence.

Financialization and the virtualization of human communication are obviously intertwined: thanks to the digitalization of exchanges, finance has turned into a social virus that is spreading everywhere, transforming things into symbols. The symbolic spiral of financialization is sucking down and swallowing up the world of physical things, of concrete skills and knowledge. The concrete wealth of Europeans is vanishing into a black hole of pure financial destruction. Nothing is created from this destruction, while the financial class is expropriating the outcome of the general labor force and of the general intellect.

Jean Baudrillard likened the ever growing US national debt to a missile orbiting above the earthly atmosphere.

An electronic billboard in Times Square displays the American public debt, an astronomic figure of some thousands of billions of dollars which increases at a rate of $20,000 a second. [...] In fact, the debt will never be paid. No debt will ever be paid. The final counts will never take place. [...] The United States is already virtually unable to pay, but this will have no consequence whatsoever. There will be no judgment day for this virtual bankruptcy. [...] When one looks at the billboard on Broadway, with its flying figures, one has the impression that the debt takes off to reach the stratosphere. This is simply the figure in light years of a galaxy that vanishes in the cosmos. The speed of liberation of the debt is just like one of earth's satellites. That's exactly what it is: the debt circulates on its own orbit, with its own trajectory made up of capital, which, from now on, is free of any economic contingency and moves about in a parallel universe (the acceleration of capital has exonerated money of its involvements with the everyday universe of production, value and utility). It is not even an orbital universe: it is rather ex-orbital, ex-centered, ex-centric, with only a very faint probability that, one day, it might rejoin ours. (Baudrillard 1996)

In the last few years, contrary to Baudrillard's prediction, the probability that he considered very faint has become true. Debt has come back down to Earth, and it is now acting as a condition for the final predatory abstraction: life turned into time for repaying a metaphysical debt. Life, intelligence, joy, breathing—humanity is going to be sacrificed in order to pay the metaphysical debt.

In the last decades of the century that trusted in the future, marked by the political hegemony of neoliberal dogma, the invisible hand has been embedded in the global technology of the linguistic machine, and language, the essential environment of mankind, has been turned into a wired, automated system.

The essential processes of social communication and production have escaped the capacities of human knowledge and control. Irreversible trends of devastation, pollution, and impoverishment are marking the horizon of our time.

Slavoj Žižek reminds us that no end of the world is in sight, only the possible end of capitalism that we are unable to imagine. Žižek may be right, but we should consider the eventuality that capitalism has so deeply pervaded every physical and imaginary dimension of the world that its collapse may lead to the end of civilization itself.

The financialization of the economy is essentially to be seen as a process of the subsumption of the processes of communication and production by the linguistic machine. The economy has been invaded by immaterial semiotic flows and transformed into a process of linguistic exchange; simultaneously, language has been captured by the digital-financial machine, and transformed into a recombination of connective operational segments. The techno-linguistic machine that is the financial web is acting as a living organism, and its mission is drying up the world.

I want to understand the process of dissolution that is underway from the unusual point of view of the relationship between poetry and finance. What has poetry to do with finance, and finance with poetry? Nothing, of course. Investors, stockholders, and bankers are usually too busy, so they don't waste their time with poetry. Poets are too poor to invest money in the stock market. There are exceptions, like T. S. Eliot, who was employed at the Lloyds Bank while writing *The Waste Land*, but this is not my point. → poor attempt at wit

My point here concerns the deterritorialization effect which has separated words from their semiotic referents and money from economic goods.

Let's consider the effect of dereferentialization which is the main thread of twentieth century poetic research (beginning with the symbolist *dérèglement des sens et des mots*), and we'll find some similarities with the economic reconfiguration that occurred during the last three decades of the century, from the neoliberal deregulation to the monetarist abstract reregulation.

Because of the technological revolution produced by information technology, the relation between time and value has been deregulated. Simultaneously, the relation between the sign and the thing has blurred, as the ontological guarantee of meaning based on the referential status of the signifier has broken apart. ↑ semiotic grounds. crisis of

"Deregulation" is a word that was first proposed by the poet Arthur Rimbaud, and later recycled as a metaphor by neoliberal ideologues. *Dérèglement des sens et des mots* is the spiritual skyline of late modern poetry. Words and senses wanted to escape the frame of representation, of denotation, and of naturalistic reproduction. So the word and the senses started to invent a new world of their own, rather than reflect or reproduce existing reality.

Neoliberal ideology starts from the same emphasis on deregulation and the cult of freedom.

The similarity between poetical and financial deregulation is misleading, of course, but powerful.

Neoliberal ideology does not intend deregulation as the free flight of social molecules out of any kind of rule, but it aims to liberate social activity from any regulation except the regulation of money, and from the rule of competition, which is the most ferocious.

Here is my point. While liberating it from the bonds of political government, financial capitalism is subjecting social behavior to techno-linguistic governance.

Governance is a keyword in the process of the financialization of the world.

Pure functionality without meaning. Automation of thought and will.

The embedding of abstract connections in the relation between living organisms.

The technical subjection of choices to the logic of concatenation.

The recombination of compatible (compatibilized) fragments (fractals).

The inscription of a digital rhythm into the social body.

In neoliberal parlance, deregulation means liberation from the constraints generated by conscious will, but simultaneously submission to techno-linguistic automatisms.

[handwritten annotation:] deregulation.
[handwritten annotation:] autonomy / conscious will ⟶ automatizm

Mathematical Ferocity and Symbolic Insolvency

Like the impressionist painters, the symbolist poets also said: "I do not want to show the thing, I want to show the impression."

The symbolists invite the reader to forget about the referent. The symbolist word is not intended to represent the thing, but to evoke a world from the imagination.

The symbolist word is intended to act as an epiphany, an apparition from nothing. I say the rose, and the rose is there, not because it is a represented referent, but because it is the effect of an act of my voice. It is the effect of a pragmatic displacement of expectations.

In symbolist poetry meaning does not come from the representation of preexisting reality and from a correspondence with the referent, but from the evocative force of sound, and voice, and rhythm.

The dereferentialization of language—the emancipation of the linguistic sign from the referent—that was the operation of symbolism, and that was the hallmark of poetic and artistic experimentation with language in the twentieth century, has something to do with a transformation in the relation between the economy and monetary exchange that occured in the last part of the century.

In 1972, Richard Nixon did something that can be considered "dereferentialization" in the realm of monetary economy. Breaking the Bretton Woods agreements, the American president said that the dollar would have no reference to reality, and that its value would henceforth be decided by an act of language, not by correspondence to a standard or to an economic referent.

Nixon's decision was the starting point of the financialization of the economy, based on the emancipation of the financial dynamic from any conventional standard and from any economic reality.

We may assert that neoliberal dictatorship began when the Chicago Boys decreed that money invented reality, when monetary evaluation foreclosed the referent. *Forget about the referent, money will create the world*—this is the arrogant declaration, of the omnipotence of economic power, which founded neoliberal monetarism.

As the economy ceases to deal with the production of things, and instead begins to evoke the world from the circulation of money, the hypertrophic growth of the debt becomes inevitable.

Neoliberal ideology pretends to be a liberating force that emancipates capital from state regulation, but it in fact submits production and social life to the most ferocious regulation, the mathematization of language.

Systematic impoverishment is imposed on social life by the logic of debt repayment. What is debt, actually? Is it an inescapable, metaphysical necessity? No. Debt is an act of language, a promise. The transformation of debt into an absolute necessity is an effect of the religion of neoliberalism, which is leading the contemporary world towards barbarianism and social devastation. → this escalated fast.

The premise of neoliberal dogmatism is the reduction of social life to the mathematical implications of financial algorithms. What is good for finance must be good for society, and if society does not accept this identification and submission, then that means that society is incompetent, and needs to be redressed by some technical authority. Goldman Sachs consultants, or bankers—like Lucas Papademous of Greece and Mario Monti of Italy—are imposed by financial power as unquestionable leaders of those countries which lag behind the necessary submission to the technical authority of statistics, algorithms, and figures, which don't want to conceive of the general interest in mathematics, or believe that social life must be submitted to the unquestionable rationale of the markets.

When democratic rituals endanger the execution of the austerity plans which are destined to restore the mathematical perfection of social life, and to pay the infinite debt that we owe to the banks, democracy is cancelled—as happened in Greece when the democratically elected President Papandreou dared to call for a referendum on the austerity measures imposed by the European banking system. Markets expelled the democratically elected Greek president, and replaced him overnight with a Goldman Sachs consultant.

What is the whimsical, supercilious entity which is often nervously referred to as "the markets"?

Markets are the visible manifestation of the inmost mathematical interfunctionality of algorithms embedded in the techno-linguistic machine: they utter sentences that change the destiny of the living body of society, destroy resources, and swallow the energies of the collective body like a draining pump.

Financial enunciations pretend to abide by the rules of indexicality. The rating agencies which downgrade or upgrade an enterprise, a bank, or a nation pretend to act as indicators of the real situation of that enterprise, that bank, or that country. They pretend to predict something about the future of that enterprise, bank, or country. Actually, they rather utter a self-fulfilling prophecy. The falsely predictive enunciations of these agencies are in reality illocutionary acts (performative utterances), social communications that have been submitted to the techno-linguistic implications of the economy.

Contemporary science and epistemology are totally at odds with the reductionist methodology of the financial economy.

The faith in the financial balance which is imposed on the European population is based on a philosophical misunderstanding: the promoters of financial stability think that the social body and mathematics belong to the same sphere. They are wrong, as reality is not mathematical, and mathematics is not the law of reality, but a language whose consistency has nothing to do with the multilayered consistency of life.

Mathematics is not in itself ferocious. Mathematics becomes ferocious when it is forcibly inscribed into the living organism of society, and this ferocious mathematization of the living body of society is preparing the worst evolution of Europe.

It should be ludicrous to say that Goldman Sachs consultants, or the European Central Bank director, or the chancellor of Germany, are Nazis. They don't look like sadistic murderers, but they want to peacefully submit the European population to mathematical slavery, which is clean, smooth, perfect.

In this way they are simultaneously establishing a cold form of totalitarianism, and preparing a hot form of massive fascist reaction. The abstract, cold violence of deterritorialized financial dictatorship is preparing the violent reterritorialization of the reactive body of European society: nation, race, ethnic cleansing, and religious fundamentalism are reappearing on the scene.

The algorithmic chain has an intrinsic causality, which is the consistent causality of a language created by the human mind in a sphere of self-validating (tautological) abstraction. The financial religion is transferring the consistency of the algorithmic chain into the social reality of the collective body. This is the philosophical misunderstanding which corresponds to the economic interests of the postbourgeois class of financial predators.

Imposing mathematical causality on the uncertainty of the bodily and social processes of becoming-other is the most dangerous of mistakes. It is provoking the birth of a new form of fascism, which is already underway in many countries of Europe, as more and more people are turning toward racist sentiments, and a wave of depression, despair, and suicide is sweeping the continent. The subjection of social communication to the financial algorithmic chain can be described as the imposition of a symbolic debt.

From this perspective, we can argue that the disentanglement of social life from the ferocious domination of mathematical exactitude is a poetic task, as poetry is language's excess: an insolvent enunciation in the face of the symbolic debt.

The Dystopic Prophecy of Poetry

The parallel histories of poetry and finance may be retraced starting from the concept of the "hyperreality of floating values," as Baudrillard put it in his seminal *Symbolic Exchange and Death* in 1976.

From symbolism to futurism, up to the experiences of the beat generation and fluxus, poets have anticipated and predicted the trajectory of the global economy and of the ordinary business of life. It has mostly been a frantic anticipation, a dystopic prophecy, as poets forebode the coming distortions and perversions of the huge deterritorialization that would come with capitalist globalization.

Think of "The Second Coming" by William Butler Yeats:

> *Turning and turning in the widening gyre*
> *The falcon cannot hear the falconer;*
> *Things fall apart; the centre cannot hold;*
> *Mere anarchy is loosed upon the world,*

> *The blood-dimmed tide is loosed, and everywhere*
> *The ceremony of innocence is drowned;*
> *The best lack all conviction, while the worst*
> *Are full of passionate intensity.*

Then, he says:

> *Surely some revelation is at hand;*
> *Surely the Second Coming is at hand.*

What revelation can we read in Yeats's poem, written in 1919?

The center cannot hold, and things have fallen apart, detached from their meaning. The revelation of the century is the devastating spiral of abstraction and nihilism: abstraction of work from activity, abstraction of goods from usefulness, abstraction of time from sensuousness. Abstraction has detached the epidermis of language from the flesh of the linguistic body.

At the beginning of the second decade of the new century, as deregulated predatory capitalism is destroying the future of the planet and of social life, poetry is going to play a new game: the game of reactivating the social body.

In the streets of Europe and in the whole Mediterranean basin, young people are revolting against the brutal exploitation of their time and intelligence, and against the financial abstraction which is devastating social life. They are the precarious generation, obliged to accept exploitation and low wages, depleted of necessary resources for their education, promised a future of the endless repetition of a meaningless act of sacrifice on the altar of debt. They are simultaneously the first connected generation, the first generation of Internet natives. They are not only protesting against the gruesome effects of neoliberal rule, they are also looking for a new meaning of things, activity, and love.

The global deterritorialization of financial capitalism has spread precariousness, psychic fragility, and desolidarization. Therefore the current precarious insurrection questions the rhythmic disturbance provoked by semio-capital, and tries to overcome our existing inability to tune into a shared vibration.

THE POWER OF IMAGINATION AND THE EUROPEAN COLLAPSE

In the crucial year 1933, Julien Benda wrote the following words, in his book *Discours à la nation européenne* (Address to the European nation):

> Europe will not be the fruit of an economic transformation: it will exist only when it will adopt a certain system of moral and aesthetic values.

I want to start from these words of Benda's because I want to talk about Europeaness: what Europe is, what Europe may be, what Europe cannot be. I start from Julien Benda and from this well-known speech on the European nation, because what is remarkable in his text is his being conscious of the fact that Europe is not an existing entity, but something that has to be created by the imagination.

What has Europe been over the past century? First of all, Europe has been the project of going beyond war, going beyond a cultural and philosophical war, not only the war between France and Germany, but the war between romanticism and Enlightenment. So, at the beginning of the twentieth century, the European project was essentially a project of the will, spirit, and imagination, if you will. Then in the 1970s and '80s, the project of Europe became a project of overcoming the opposition between East and West, between democracy and existing socialism, and so on—a project that existed in the imagination of Europeans.

What now? This is the question I'm trying to answer. What is Europe now? If we listen to the speeches of Angela Merkel, for instance, and to those of all the other European politicians, be they leftist or rightist, it makes no difference… Europe is a dogmatic project of reassuming and reinforcing neoliberal ideology, of a neoliberal regulation that leads to the impoverishment of European societies: to the slashing of salaries, to the postponement of retirement, and finally, to the sad project of destroying, of devastating, of dismantling the general intellect.

This is the central project of Europe nowadays: the destruction of collective intelligence. Or, if you want to say it in a more prosaic way, the destruction of the university, and the subjugation of research to the narrow interests of profit and economic competition.

You know the situation of our most recent generation of students, for instance: we are teaching things that may be good or bad, but are in the end useless as far as their future is concerned, because they don't have a future.

Not having a future: this is already a kind of refrain, but I think we should start from this consideration, from this obvious knowledge—the idea of a nonexistent future—as a condition of thought: if we start by dismantling the very possibility of a future, we are obliged to go beyond the dogmatic reassertion of neoliberalism.

Let us look at the landscape of philosophical and political thought in Europe today, the so-called European high culture. The landscape is rather gloomy.

I remember what the philosophical discussion was in the 1960s and '70s, in the wake of the

Critical Theory that made possible the creation of the European entity in the sphere of dialectical thought.

I remember what French thought was in the 1970s and in the '80s, in the age of Gilles Deleuze and Félix Guattari, Michel Foucault, Jacques Derrida, and Jean-François Lyotard. Their thought was an attempt to imagine a possible future, but it was also much more: it offered a cartography of the coming future of the neoliberal, self-proclaimed deregulation.

I think, for instance, of Foucault's wonderful book, *The Birth of Biopolitics*, which was probably the most enlightening, imaginative forewarning of what was going to happen in the landscape of the world.

And I also think of books like *Anti-Oedipus* and *A Thousand Plateaus*, and Baudrillard's *Symbolic Exchange and Death*. These are the most important books of the 1970s and '80s, and you can read them all as cautionary imaginations of the coming neoliberal revolution. The work of these French philosophers of the 1970s and '80s has formulated a cartography of the coming dystopia: a way of thinking about the coming future as a dark age of violence and impoverishment.

Then I look at the landscape of German philosophy in the 1970s and '80s: I consider the debate between Jürgen Habermas and Niklas Luhmann, for instance. This, too, was an important anticipation of what Europe was going to become.

The good and, in a sense, benevolent idea of the Habermasian dialogic society, on the one side: the predicted benefits of communication, the deceptive illusion of communication based in democracy. And, on the other side, the realistic consideration of Luhmann, who described a future without alternatives, without possible utopias, a future of governance. This was a high-profile discussion, which was focusing the real, problematic horizon of the European future.

Governance, this word which has totally invaded the field of political nonthought, was first proposed and deconstructed by Luhmann in the 1970s and '80s. What is the meaning of this word, beyond the political manipulations of the ruling class over the last few decades?

As far as I can understand, the fact that *governance* is a word which is much used and never defined today is a symptom of the total poverty of the political practice of our time.

If we begin from the Luhmannian perspective, we can understand that governance is the automation of thought, the automation of social existence. Governance is information without meaning, a dominance of the unavoidable.

In governance praxis, economic dogma is transformed into techno-linguistic automatism.

This is governance at its very end. In this sense, Luhmann was kind of like a Philip K. Dick of political thought; he was like the Johnny Rotten of political imagination. He was speaking about *no future*, the coming no future, which is the here and now.

Starting from this sense of no future that the political thought of the 1970s and '80s had proclaimed and mapped in advance, we can understand what is happening today in the present European nightmare.

Those thinkers were able to imagine and to criticize, but now? Now, cynicism has invaded the sphere of thought, no less than the sphere of politics.

Look at the sadness of French cynical thought, think of what has become of the intellectual landscape of Paris: a monument to sadness, a monument to cynicism. Paris today is a city where thought has been transformed into journalism, into the continuous repetition of this kind of illusion of European arrogance which has paved the way to the financial collapse, to the infinite war that George W. Bush has proclaimed, and that Tony Blair, Nicolas Sarkozy, José Maria Aznar, and Silvio Berlusconi have supported.

The cynical nonthinkers who inhabit the Parisian scene of today, once called *les nouveaux philosophes*, have paved the way to dogmatism, violence, racism, impoverishment, and financial dictatorship.

A light of possible intelligence and openness seems to come not from philosophy, but from art.

I am not actually sure of what I am talking about when I say the word *art*. You aren't either—nobody is exactly.

Yet it seems that in a recent poll, twenty-four to twenty-five percent of young German people interviewed by journalists answered the question "what do you want to do when you're an adult" by stating that they wanted to be artists. What are they picturing? What do they think being an artist means, exactly? Are they thinking about the rich possibilities that the art market offers? Well, maybe, but I don't think so. I think that they are saying that they want to be artists because they feel that being an artist means to escape a future of sadness, to escape a future of precariousness as sadness. They are thinking, well, precariousness and sadness can become something different, something not so sad, not so precarious, if they withdraw their faith, if they withdraw from any expectations a capitalist future can offer. I don't want to expect anything from the future, so I start my future as an artist.

"The German worker does not want to pay the Greek fisherman's bills." The fanatics of economic fundamentalism are pitting workers against workers and leading Europe to the brink of civil war. In their relentless efforts to transfer money and resources from society to the financial classes, neoliberal ideologues have never hesitated to use manipulation and deception: their half-truths and fictions are transformed by the global media into "common knowledge." Here are a few such conceptual manipulations which are helping neoliberalism destroy European society:

First manipulation: *By lowering taxes on the rich, you will increase employment.*

Why should this be the case? Such logic is beyond comprehension. On the contrary: the owners of capital invest only so long as their profits are perceived to be guaranteed. Any influence of state taxation on investment plans is at best inconsequential, and more often than not irrelevant. The state should thus progressively increase taxation on the rich in order to further invest resources and create jobs. The conceptual foundation of Reaganomics, the so-called Laffer curve (progressive lowering of taxes on the affluent), is nothing more than abstract rubbish which has been transformed into a legislative commandment wielded by both the left and right wings for the last thirty years.

Second manipulation: *Postponing the retirement age increases youth employment.*

An absurd assessment. If an elderly worker retires, logically a new job will be available for a younger worker. If, however, an elderly worker is forced to work an additional five, six, or seven years beyond what was stipulated in his contract, logically this job will not be available for a younger worker throughout the entirety of the additional duration. A simple syllogism. Yet economic policy over the last thirty years, both on the left and right wings, favors this mysterious and contradictory principle in which elderly workers must be forced to work longer in order to increase employment opportunities for the young. The result being that capitalists, instead of paying a pension to the elderly and a salary to young workers, pay a single salary to overaged workers while blackmailing unemployed youths into accepting any form whatsoever of precarious, underpaid labor.

Third manipulation: *Privatization and market competition are the best guarantees of quality for schools and public services.*

Over thirty years of rampant privatization has amply demonstrated that the private sector inherently facilitates drastic reductions in quality. This is because the private sector is primarily interested in increasing profits, not promoting the public good. And when reduction in quality leads to outright malfunction, as often happens, the resulting losses for prerequisite services are socialized while profits remain private.

Fourth manipulation: *Workers are paid too much— we have been living above and beyond our means. We must be paid less in order to become more competitive.*

The preceding decades have witnessed a drastic cut in actual wages, while profits have skyrocketed. In successfully leveraging the threat of job transfer to newly industrialized countries where the cost of work hovers at near-slavery levels and conditions, western workers' salaries have been severely reduced along with the capitalist's production costs. Debt has been favored in any and all forms in order to entice people to purchase otherwise unsellable merchandise and goods. All of this has induced a cultural and political process of pushing forms of social agency into a condition of dependency (debt is an agent within the unconscious enabling guilt and a consequent drive for atonement), and at the same time has rendered the entire societal system vulnerable and fragile, exposing it to repeated collapse as witnessed in the frequent economic bubble "boom and crash" cycles.

Fifth manipulation: *Inflation is our preeminent danger, and the Central European Bank has only one goal, to oppose inflation at any cost.*

What is inflation? Inflation is either a reduction in the value of money, or an increase in the price of commodities. Inflation may indeed be dangerous for a society, but balancing mechanisms may be put into place (such as the sliding-scale mechanism used in Italy until 1984, when it was cancelled under yet another glorious neoliberal "reform"). The true danger for social life is deflation, which leads to recession and the reduction of the social machine's productive potential. Owners of capital, rather than seeing the value of their money diminish, prefer provoking recession and widespread social misery. The European bank prefers creating recession, misery, unemployment, poverty, barbarianism, and violence, rather than abdicating the restrictive rules of the Maastricht Treaty, which prevent it from easily printing money, giving society space to breathe, and redistributing wealth. In order to manufacture an artificial fear of inflation, the ghost of Germany's inflation cycle of the 1920s (justly feared by the Germans) is invoked, as if inflation itself were the cause of Nazism, and not the manner in which inflation was managed by German and international capitalists of the time.

Everything is crumbling—it's crystal clear. The measures that the financial class are forcing on European countries are the exact opposite of "solutions": they can only multiply the scale and effects of the disaster. It's called a financial "rescue," but it's a strange form of rescue, designed to slash salaries (thereby reducing future demand), cut spending on social infrastructure, destroy public schools, and contract present and future productive capacity, thereby inducing an immediate recession. The way events have unfolded in Greece perfectly demonstrates these facts: the European financial rescue has destroyed its productive capacity, privatized its public structures, and demoralized its population. Greece's Gross Domestic Product has dropped by seven percent in one year alone, with no signs of recovery. Rescue loans are administered at such high rates of interest that Greece can only sink further into debt and endure an increasing sense of guilt, misery, and hatred toward Europe. And now the Greek "rescue" is being applied to Portugal, Spain, Ireland, and Italy. Its only effect will be a massive transfer of resources and wealth from these countries to the ruling financial class. Austerity will not reduce deficits. On the contrary, it will lead to deflation, as well as the reduction of production and wealth, provoking further debt and consequent borrowing to the point where the European castle will be forced to crumble.

Resistance movements must be prepared. Revolt is winding its way through European cities, having taken concrete shape in Rome, Athens, and London on December 14, 2010; and later in the *acampada* protests of May and June in Spain, and the four nights of rage in the suburbs of England. Insurrection will expand and proliferate in the upcoming months, yet it will not be a lighthearted undertaking, nor will it be a linear process of social emancipation.

Society has been broken up, rendered fragile and fragmented by thirty years of perpetual precarization, uncontrolled and rampant competition, and psychic poisoning produced and controlled by the likes of Rupert Murdoch, Silvio Berlusconi, and their criminal media empires.

There will be little cheer in the coming insurrection, which will often be marked by racism and self-defeating violence. This is the unfortunate effect of the long process of desolidarization which neoliberalism and the criminal political left have subjected society to for decades through their incessant proliferation and fragmentation of work.

In the upcoming years we can expect the diffusion of widespread ethnic civil war, as already witnessed in the dust of the English revolt and the outbursts of violence in Birmingham. No one will be able to stop or guide the insurrection, which will function as a chaotic reactivation of the energies of the body of the socius, which has for too long been flattened, fragmented, and lobotomized. The task of resistance movements will not be to provoke, but rather to create (coextensively with the insurrection) autonomous structures for knowledge, existence, survival, psychotherapy, and giving life meaning and ~~autonomy~~. This will be a long and potentially traumatic process.

Europe must overcome Maastricht in order to be reinvented. Debt must be disowned just as must be the measures which cause and feed it. The fall of Maastricht is perilous, yet unavoidable, as it will inevitably open the doors to nationalism and violence. Yet Europe, as it stands, can no longer be defended. Resistance movements must rearticulate European discourse through social solidarity, egalitarianism, the reduction of working time, the expropriation of capital conglomerates, the cancellation of debt, and the abolition of borders toward the construction of a postterritorial politics. Europe must be pushed beyond Maastricht and the Schengen Agreement and embrace a future form of the international.

THE RIGHT TO INSOLVENCY AND THE DISENTANGLE-MENT OF THE POTENCY OF THE GENERAL INTELLECT

A Movement for the Reactivation of the Social Body

The European leading class seems incapable of thinking in terms of the future. They are panicking and, frightened by their own impotence, they are trying to reaffirm and reinforce measures that have already failed.

The European collapse is exposing the agony of capitalism. The flexibility of the system is over, no margins are left. If society is to pay the debt of the banks, demand has to be reduced, and if demand is reduced, growth will not follow.

Nowadays, it's difficult to see a consistent project in the frantic action of the leading class. "No future" culture has taken hold of the capitalist brain, and the origin of this capitalist nihilism is to be found in the effect of deterritorialization that is inherent to global financial capitalism. The relation between capital and society is deterritorialized, as economic power is no longer based on the property of physical things. The bourgeoisie is dead, and the new financial class has a virtual existence: fragmented, dispersed, impersonal.

The bourgeoisie, which was once in control of the economic scene of modern Europe, was a strongly territorialized class, linked to material assets; it could not survive without relationships to territory and community. The financial class which has taken the reins of the European political machine has no attachment either to territory or to material production, because its power and wealth are founded on the total abstraction of digital finance. This digital-financial hyperabstraction is liquidating the living body of the planet and the social body of the workers' community.

Can it last? The European directorate that emerged after the Greek crisis, in the absence of any consultation of public opinion, has affirmed its own monopoly over decisions regarding the economies of the different countries approaching default in 2011. It effectively divested parliaments of authority and replaced EU democracy with a business executive headed by the large banks. Can the ECB-IMF-EU directorate impose a system of automatisms that secures EU members' compliance with the process of public-sector wage reduction, layoffs of a third of all teachers, and so on? This order of things can not last indefinitely, as the final collapse of the Union is the point of arrival of the spiral of debt-deflation-recession-debt that is already exposed in the Greek agony.

Society was slow in reacting, as collective intelligence has been deprived of its social body, and the social body has been completely subjugated and depressed. Then, at the end of 2010, a wave of protests and riots exploded in the schools and universities, and now that wave is mounting everywhere. But protests, demonstrations, and riots seem unable to force a change in the politics of the Union. Let's try to understand why, and let's also try to look for a new methodology of action and a new political strategy for the movement.

The protest movement has proliferated during the last year. From London to Rome, from Athens to New York, not to mention the North African precarious workers who have been part of the recent upheavals that are changing (for better or worse) the Arab world, this movement is targeting the financial powers and trying to oppose the effects of the financial assault on society. The problem is that peaceful demonstrations and protests have not been able to change the agenda of the European Central Bank, as the national parliaments of the European countries are hostages of the Maastricht rules, which are financial automatisms working as the material constitution of the Union. Peaceful demonstrations are effective in the frame of democracy, but democracy is over now that techno-financial automatisms have taken the place of political decisions.

Violence is erupting here and there. The four nights of rage in the English suburbs and the violent riots of Rome and Athens have shown that it's possible for social protest to become aggressive. But violence, too, is unfit to change the course of things. Burning a bank is totally useless, as financial power is not in the physical buildings, but in the abstract connections between numbers, algorithms, and information. Therefore, if we want to discover forms of action which may be able to confront the present form of power, we have to start from the understanding that cognitive labor is the main productive force creating the techno-linguistic automatisms which enable financial speculation. Following the example of Wikileaks, we must organize a long-lasting process of dismantling and rewriting the techno-linguistic automatons enslaving all of us.

Social subjectivity seems weak and fragmented against the backdrop of the financial assault. Thirty years of the precarization of labor and competition have jeopardized the very fabric of social solidarity, and workers' psychic ability to share time, goods, and breath made fragile. The virtualization of social communication has eroded the empathy between human bodies.

The problem of solidarity has always been crucial in every process of struggle and social change.

Autonomy is based on the ability to share daily life and to recognize that what is good for me is good for you, and that what is bad for you is bad for me. Solidarity is difficult to build now that labor has been turned into a sprawl of recombinant time-cells, and now that the process of subjectivation has consequently become fragmentary, disempathetic, and frail.

Solidarity has nothing to do with altruistic self-denial. In materialistic terms, solidarity is not about you, it's about me. Like love, solidarity is not about altruism: it is about the pleasure of sharing

this logic is killing

the breath and space of the other. Love is the ability to enjoy myself thanks to your presence, to your eyes. This is solidarity. Because solidarity is based on the territorial proximity of social bodies, you cannot build solidarity between fragments of time.

I don't think that the English riots and the Italian revolts and the Spanish *acampada* should be seen as consequential revolutionary forms, because they are unable to really strike at the heart of power. They have to be understood as forms of the psycho-affective reactivation of the social body; they have to be seen as attempts to activate a living relation between the social body and the general intellect. Only when the general intellect is able to reconnect with the social body will we be able to start a process of real autonomization from the grip of financial capitalism.

The Right to Insolvency

A new concept is emerging from the fog of the present situation: the right to insolvency. We're not going to pay the debt.

The European countries have been obliged to accept the blackmail of the debt, but people are rejecting the notion that we should have to pay for a debt that we have not taken.

Anthropologist David Graeber, in his book *Debt: The First 5,000 Years* (2011), and philosopher

Maurizio Lazzarato, in *The Making of the Indebted Man* (2012), have inaugurated an interesting reflection on the cultural origin of the notion of debt, and the psychic implications of the sense of guilt that this notion carries.

Additionally, in his essay "Recurring Dreams— The Red Heart of Fascism," the young Anglo-Italian thinker Federico Campagna pinpoints the analogy between the post-Versailles Congress years and the debt-obsessed present.

> Last time, it took him decades to be born. First it was the war, and then, once it was over, it was debt, and all the ties that came with it. It was the time of industrialization, the time of modernity, and everything came in a mass scale. Mass impoverishment, mass unemployment, hyper-inflation, hyper-populism. Nations were cracking under the weight of what marxists used to call "contradictions," while capitalists were clinging to the brim of their top-hats, all waiting for the sky to fall to earth. And when it fell, they threw themselves down after it, in the dozens, down from their skyscrapers and their office blocks. The air became electric, squares filled up, trees turned into banners and batons. It was the inter-war period, and in the depth of the social body, Nazism was still hidden, liquid and growing, quiet like a foetus.

This time, everything is happening almost exactly the same way as last time, just slightly out-of-sync, as happens with recurring dreams. Once again, the balance of power in the world is shifting. The old empire is sinking, melancholically, and new powers are rushing in the race to the top. Just like before, their athletic screams are the powerful ones of modernity. Growth! Growth! Growth! Their armies are powerful, their teeth shiny, their hopes murderous and pure. Old powers look at them in fear, listening to their incomprehensible languages like old people listen to young people's music. (Campagna, 2011)

The burden of debt is haunting the European imagination of the future, and the Union, which used to represent a promise of prosperity and peace, is turning into a blackmail and a threat.

In response, the movement has launched the slogan: *We're not going to pay the debt.* These words are deceiving at the moment, as in actuality we are already paying for the debt: the educational system has already been definanced and privatized, jobs have been elimated, and so on. But these words are meant to change the social perception of the debt, creating a consciousness of its arbitrariness and moral illegitimacy.

The right to insolvency is emerging as a new key phrase and concept loaded with philosophical implications. The concept of insolvency implies not only a refusal to pay the financial debt, but also, in a more subtle way, a refusal to submit the living potency of social forces to the formal domination of the economic code.

The reclamation of the right to insolvency implies a radical questioning of the relation between the capitalist form (Gestalt) and the concrete productive potency of social forces, particularly the potency of the general intellect. The capitalist form is not only a set of economic rules and functions, it is also the internalization of a certain set of limitations, of psychic automatism, of rules for compliance.

Try to imagine for a second that the whole financial semiotization of European life disappears; try to imagine that all of a sudden we stop organizing daily life in terms of money and debt. Nothing would change in the concrete, useful potentiality of society, in the contents of our knowledge, in our skills and ability to produce.

We should imagine (and consequently organize) the disentanglement of the living potentiality of the general intellect from the capitalist Gestalt—intended, first and foremost, as a psychic automatism governing daily life.

Insolvency means disclaiming the economic code of capitalism as a transliteration of real life, as a semiotization of social potency and richness.

The concrete, useful productive ability of the social body is forced to accept impoverishment in exchange for nothing. The concrete force of productive labor is submitted to the unproductive, and actually destructive, task of refinancing the failed financial system.

If we may paradoxically cancel every mark of this financial semiotization, nothing would change in the social machinery, nothing in our intellectual ability to conceive and perform.

Communism does not need to be called out from the womb of the future; it is here, in our being, in the immanent life of common knowledge.

But the present situation is paradoxical— simultaneously exciting and despairing. Capitalism has never been so close to its final collapse, but social solidarity has never been so far from our daily experience. We must start from this paradox in order to build a postpolitical and postrevolutionary process of disentangling the possible from the existent.

EXHAUSTION: A SENILE UTOPIA FOR THE EUROPEAN INSURRECTION

Financial Dictatorship

Intellectuals like Jürgen Habermas and Jacques Derrida, among many others, have in the past stressed the refrain: "We need to create institutions for unified political decision at the level of the European Union."

In the aftermath of the Greek crisis, it seems that the Europhile intellectuals have gotten what they have been asking for. The Euro entity has been subjected to an act of political decision and to a sort of political directorate which is enforcing narrow obedience. Unfortunately, however, politics has taken this lead only in order to make the assessment that finance alone represents the true leadership of the Union.

A political enforcement of finance's domination over European society has been the outcome so far of this early stage of the European tragedy.

Welfare-state institutions have been under attack for thirty years. Full employment, labor rights, social security, retirement, public school, public transportation—all have been reduced, worsened, or destroyed. After thirty years of neoliberal zeal, a collapse has occurred.

What will happen next? The leading class answers roughly: more of the same. Further reduction of salaries for public workers, further postponement of the retirement age. No respect for society's needs or for the rights of workers.

Thatcher said thirty years ago that there is no such thing as society. Today, that echoes like a self-fulfilling prophecy. Society is in fact dissolving, reducing public space to a jungle wherein everyone is fighting against one another. After the Greek crisis, the dogma of monetarism has been strongly reinforced, as if more poison could act as an antidote. Reducing demand will lead to recession, and the only outcome will be a further concentration of capital in the hands of the financial class, and the further impoverishment of labor.

positive feedback

After the Greek financial crisis, emergency rule was declared. A self-proclaimed directorate, Merkel-Sarkozy-Trichet, imposed a deflationary policy, and is now going to impose it on the different national governments of Europe. In order to save the financial system, this self-proclaimed directorate is diverting resources from society to the banks. And in order to reaffirm the failed philosophy of neoliberalism, social spending is cut, salaries are lowered, retirement time is postponed, and young people's work is made precarious.

Those who will not bend to the Great Necessity (Competition and Growth) will be out of the game. Those who want to stay in the game will have to accept any punishment, any renunciation, any suffering that the Great Necessity will demand. Who said that we absolutely must be part of the game?

The effect of the collapse of neoliberal politics has so far been its own confirmation and consolidation. After the collapse of the American financial system, everybody was expecting abandonment or at least attenuation of capital concentration, and a process of revenue redistribution seemed possible in order to increase demand. Nothing like this has happened. A Keynesian approach has not even been explored, and Paul Krugman has been left alone to repeat very reasonable things that nobody wants to hear.

Thanks to the crisis, American society has been robbed for the benefit of big finance, and now Europe is following the same dynamic, with a sort of mathematical ferocity.

Is there any chance of stopping this insane race?

A social explosion is possible, because the conditions of daily life will soon become unbearable. But labor precarity and the decomposition of social solidarity may open the way to a frightening outcome: ethnic civil war on a continental scale and the dismantling of the Union, which would unleash the worst passions of the nations.

In Paris, London, Barcelona, and Rome, massive demonstrations have erupted in protest against the restrictive measures, but this movement is not going to stop the catastrophic freight train of aggression bearing down on social life, because the European Union is not a democracy but rather a financial dictatorship whose politics is subjected to unquestionable decisions.

Peaceful demonstrations will not be able to change the course of things, and predictable violent explosions will be exploited by the repressive force of the state. A deep change in social perception and lifestyle will occur, and a growing portion of society will withdraw from the economic field, and stop partaking in the game of work and consumption. These people will abandon the script of individual consumption; create new, enhanced forms of cohabitation; establish village economies in metropolises; withdraw from the field of the market economy; and create community currencies.

Unless they are seized by avarice—a psychotic obsession—all that human beings want is a pleasant, possibly long life, and to consume only what is necessary to stay fit and make love. "Civilization" is the pompous name we have given to every political and moral value that has made the pursuit of such a lifestyle possible.

The financial dogma states the following: if we want to keep participating in the game played in banks and stock markets, we must forfeit a pleasant, quiet life. We must forfeit civilization. But why should we accept this exchange? Europe's wealth is not based on the stability of the euro on international markets, or on managers' ability to keep count of their profits. Europe is wealthy because it has millions of intellectuals, scientists, technicians, doctors, and poets, and millions of workers who have for centuries developed technical knowledge. Europe is wealthy because it has *wow*

historically managed to valorize competence, not just competition, and to welcome and integrate cultures from afar. It is also wealthy, it must be said, because for four centuries it has ferociously exploited the physical and human resources of other continents.

We must forfeit something, but what exactly?

Certainly, we must let go of the hyperconsumption imposed on us by large corporations—but not by the traditions of humanism, the Enlightenment, and socialism, not by the ideals of freedom, civil rights, and welfare. And I say this not because I believe we should be attached to principles of the past, but because these principals make it possible to live decently.

The prospect open to us is not a revolution. The concept of revolution no longer corresponds to anything, because it entails an exaggerated notion of political will over the complexity of contemporary society. Our prospect is a paradigmatic shift: to a new paradigm that is not centered on product growth, profit, and accumulation, but on the full, unfolding of the power of collective intelligence.

Aesthetics of Europe

The aesthetics of the European Union are frigid by definition.

The European Union was born in the aftermath of the Second World War, with the goal of forgetting our old nationalist and ideological passions. Here lies its progressive and pragmatic nature. Forgetting romanticism is the categorical imperative of the Union.

Lately, however, this foundational, antimythological myth of the Union seems blurred, confused, and forgotten because its apathetic perception of being together was only possible in a condition of prosperity. As long as the EU was able to guarantee a growing level of consumption, as long as the monetarist rule favored economic growth, the EU could exist. What now?

The European Union is a fiction of democracy actually governed by an autocratic organism, the European Central Bank. While the Federal Reserve in the US is officially dedicated to the stability of prices and full employment, the ECB charter declares only one goal: fighting inflation. Today this goal is irrational, as deflation is the prevailing trend.

Citizens can do nothing in order to influence the politics of the ECB, as the Bank does not respond to political authority. This is why European citizens have been conscious of the vacuity of European elections. In the future they may come to view the Union as their enemy.

Social movements should try to change the landscape, and imagine the mythology for cultural transition. We should focus on a foundational myth of European history: the myth of energy. Modern culture and political imagination have emphasized the virtues of youth—of young passion, and of energy, aggressiveness, and growth. Capitalism is based on the exploitation of physical energy, and semio-capitalism has subjugated the nervous energy of society to the point of collapse.

The notion of exhaustion has always been anathema for the discourse of Modernity: *Romantik Sturm und Drang*, the Faustian drive toward immortality, an endless thirst for economic growth, and profits.

Organic limits have been denied, forgotten. The organic body of the Earth, and the entropy inherent to human life, has been despised, concealed, and segregated.

The romantic cult of youth is the cultural source of nationalism. During the Romantic era, Europe was an emerging civilization which was securing political hegemony by conquering the great Eastern civilizations. We should not forget that at the end of the eighteenth century, India and China were responsible for producing more than seventy percent of the total global product of the world. Their decline cannot be separated from Europe's ascent to domination.

In the colonial age, nationalism was the cultural condition of colonial Empires like Britain and

France, but around the turn of the twentieth century, nationalism resurfaced in a responsive form and began to express the self-affirmation of young countries (Italy, Japan, and Germany), while the old empires (Russia, Austria and the Ottomans) were heading toward collapse.

Nationalism can also take a self-affirmative form for the young generation at the cultural and economic level, as is evident in Italian futurism. Old-fashioned styles are devalued, old people and women despised because of their weakness. Fascism depicts itself as the young age of the nations.

In late modernity, the rhetoric of the young and the devaluation of the old becomes an essential feature of advertising. Contrary to fascist discourse, late-modern advertising does not abuse old age. It denies it, claiming that every old person can be young if they will only take part in the consumerist feast.

The fascism that triumphed in Italy after 1922 can be seen as an *energolatreia* (energy worship) of the young.

Berlusconi's style is restaging arrogance, contempt for democratic rules, and machoism, but the actors of the present comedy are old men who seek help from bio-techniques, psycho-chemistry, and pharmacology. Denial of age and of time is the ultimate delirium of the global class, as Norman Spinrad shows in his 1969 novel, *Bug Jack Barron*.

youth

Like the heroic mythology of fascist nationalism (and also the mythology of advertising), Berlusconi's subculture is based on a delirium of power. The former was based on the youthful virtues of strength, energy, and pride; the latter is based on the mature virtues of technique, deception, and finance. The nemesis that followed the youthful violence of fascism was the Second World War and its unthinkable surfeit of destruction and death. What nemesis will be brought about by the present *energolatreia* of the old?

The destiny of Europe will play out in the biopolitical sphere, at the border between consumerism, techno-sanitarian youth-styled aggressivity, and the possible collective consciousness of the limits of the biological (sensitive) organism.

Exhaustion has no place in Western culture, and this is a problem right now, because exhaustion needs to be understood and accepted as a new paradigm for social life. Only the cultural and psychic elaboration of exhaustion will open the door to a new conception and perception of wealth and happiness.

The coming European insurrection will not be an insurrection of energy, but an insurrection of slowness, withdrawal, and exhaustion. It will be the autonomization of the collective body and soul from the exploitation of speed and competition.

In the next decade, Europe will make a decisive choice. Europe now faces a dilemma between two hypotheses.

One path would be to accept a deal that redistributes wealth and resources; that opens Europe's borders to the crowds coming from Africa and Asia; that implies a reduction in the Western, comsumptive lifestyle, heading instead toward a nongrowth of production and consumption. This option would not imply the idea of sacrifice and renunciation, but rather the enjoyment of time without any expectation of competitive acquisition and accumulation.

The other would be an intensification of the interethnic civil war whose first signs are already visible. The majority of European people are desperately defending the privilege accumulated during the centuries of colonialism, but this privilege has been deteriorating since the fall of colonialist empires in the past century, and is now falling apart in the course of the global recession.

In the game of economic competition, Europe cannot win. How long will it take to reduce a typical European salary to the level of an Indian, Chinese, or Vietnamese worker? It's going to take too much time and too much violence and blood. This is why financial markets distrust the euro: if the standard is capital gain, profit, and competition, then Europe's decline is guaranteed.

The question that remains is: who says that economic competition is the only standard and political criterion of choice? Bateson would define the European malaise in terms of a double-bind, or contradictory injunction. Neoliberal dogma is dictating European society to compete, and is simultaneously dictating the destruction of the structures constituting the cultural and productive condition of its wealth. The neoliberal idea of wealth is advancing social misery more and more. Gregory Bateson suggests that double-binds have paradoxical outcomes. And the paradoxical solution for Europe could be to not fear decline. Decline (reverse growth) implies a divestment from the frenzy of competition: this is the paradoxical path that may bring us out of neoliberalism's double-bind.

2

LANGUAGE, ECONOMY, AND THE BODY

THE FUTURE AFTER THE END OF THE ECONOMY

Economic Science Is Not a Science

At the close of the summer of 2011, the economic newspapers were talking more and more of a "double dip." Economists predict there will be another recession before there can be a recovery.

I think they are wrong. There will be a recession—on that I agree—but there will never again be any recovery, if recovery means a renewal of growth.

If you say this in public, you are regarded as a traitor, a wrecker, a doomsayer, and economists scorn you as a villain. But economists are not wise people. They should not even be considered scientists. They are much more similar to priests, denouncing society's bad behaviors, asking you to repent for your debts, threatening inflation and misery for your sins, and worshipping the dogmas of growth and competition.

It is difficult to believe that something like "economic science" really exists. What is a science? Without embarking on epistemological discussions, I would simply say that science is a form of knowledge which is free of dogma, which is able to extrapolate general laws from the observation of empirical phenomena (and consequently able to predict something about what will happen next), and finally which is able to understand those kinds of changes that Thomas Kuhn has labeled paradigm shifts. → *changed criteria.*

As far as I know, the discourse named "economics" does not correspond to this schema.

First of all, economists are beset with dogmatic notions like growth, competition, and gross national product, and they determine that social reality is out of order when it is not matching these criteria.

Second, economists are totally unable to infer laws from the observation of reality, as they prefer instead that reality harmonize with their pretended laws. As a consequence, they are totally unable to predict anything, as experience has shown over the last three or four years.

Finally, economists cannot understand what is happening when the social paradigm is changing, and strongly refuse to redefine their conceptual framework because they pretend that reality has to be changed in order for it to correspond to their outdated criteria.

The faculty and students of economics and business schools do not teach and learn subjects like physics or chemistry or astronomy, disciplines that deserve the title of scientific knowledge, and which each conceptualize a specific field of reality. Economics faculty and students rather teach and study a technology, a set of tools, of procedures, of pragmatic protocols that are intended to force social reality into practical purposes: profits, accumulation, power. Economic reality does not exist, it is the result of a process of technical modeling, submission, and exploitation.

The theoretical discourse that supports the economic technology can be defined as ideology, in the sense proposed by Marx, who was not an economist, but a critic of political economy.

Ideology is in fact a theoretical technology aimed at supporting special political and social goals. And economics ideology, like all technologies, is not self-reflexive, and therefore is unable to develop a theoretical self-appreciation and to reframe itself in relation to a paradigm shift.

Financial Deterritorialization and Labor Precarity

The development of productive forces, the creation of the global network of cognitive labor that in "Fragment on Machines" (*Grundrisse*) Marx named "general intellect," has provoked an enormous increase in the productive potency of labor. This potency can no longer be semiotized, organized, and contained by the social form of capitalism.

Capitalism is no longer able to semiotize and to organize the social potency of cognitive productivity, because value can no longer be defined in terms of the average necessary time of labor, and therefore the old forms of private property and salary are no longer able to semiotize and organize the deterritorialized existence of capital and social labor.

Economists are totally dazzled by this transformation, as economic knowledge has always been structured according to the paradigm of bourgeois capitalism: linear accumulation, measurability of value, and private appropriation of surplus value. The shift from the industrial form of production to the semiotic form of production, the shift from physical labor to cognitive labor, has projected capitalism out of itself, out of its ideological self-consciousness.

The bourgeoisie, which was a territorialized class (the class of the *bourg*, of the city), was able to manage physical property, as well as a measurable relation between time and value. The utter financialization of capital marks the end of the old bourgeoisie, and opens the door to the deterritorialized and rhizomatic proliferation of economic power relations. Now the old bourgeoisie has no power anymore, having been replaced by a proliferating virtual class (a deterritorialized and pulverized social dust, rather than a territorialized group of people) that is usually referred to as "financial markets."

Labor is undergoing a parallel process of pulverization and deterritorialization, that is called precarity (or the precariousness of labor). Precarization is not only the loss of a regular job and a salary, but it is also the effect of fragmentation and pulverization of work, the fracture in the relationship between worker and territory. The cognitive worker, in fact, does not need to be linked to a place, and his or her activity can be diffused throughout a nonphysical territory.

The old economic categories (salary, private property, and linear growth) no longer make sense in this new situation. The productivity of the general intellect, in terms of use value (of production of useful semiotic goods), is virtually unlimited. So how can semiotic labor be valued, when its products are immaterial? How can the relationship between work and salary be determined? How can we measure value in terms of time, if the productivity of cognitive work (creative, affective, linguistic) cannot be quantified and standardized?

The End of Growth

The notion of growth is crucial in the conceptual framework of the economic technology. If social production does not comply with the economic expectations of growth, economists decree that society is sick and shivering, and they name the disease "recession." This diagnosis has nothing to do with the needs of the population, because it does not refer to the use-value of things and of semiotic goods, but to abstract capitalist accumulation, which is accumulation of exchange value.

Growth, in the economic sense, is not about the increase of social happiness and satisfaction of the basic needs of people, but about the expansion of financial profits and the expansion of the global volume of exchange value. Gross national product, the main indicator of growth, is not a measure of social welfare and pleasure, but a monetary measure.

Social happiness or unhappiness does not generally depend on the amount of money circulating in the economy, but rather depends on the distribution of wealth, and on the balance of cultural expectations and the availability of physical and semiotic goods.

Growth is a cultural concept, more than it is an evaluative economic criterion of social health and well being. It is linked to the modern conception of the future as infinite expansion.

For many reasons, infinite expansion has become an impossible task for the social body. Since the Club of Rome published the book *The Limits to Growth* in 1972, we have been informed that the physical resources of the planet are not boundless, and social production has to be redefined according to this knowledge.

The cognitive transformation of production and the creation of a semio-capitalist sphere have opened a new possibility for expansion—and for a few years in the 1990s the economy was able to expand euphorically, while the Internet economy was expected to furnish a new landscape of infinite growth. It was a deception, because even if the general intellect is infinitely productive, the limits to growth are inscribed in the affective body of cognitive work: limits of attention, of psychic energy, of sensibility. After the illusions of the new economy (spread by wired neoliberal ideologues) and the eventual dot-com crash, the very beginning of the new century announced the coming collapse of the financial economy. Since September 2008, we have known that (notwithstanding the financial virtualization of expansion) the end of capitalist growth is in sight.

This could be a curse, if social welfare remains dependent on the expansion of monetary profits, and if we are unable to redefine social needs and expectations. But it could become a blessing if we redistribute social product in an egalitarian way, if we share existing resources, and if we revise our cultural expectations to be more frugal, replacing the idea that pleasure depends on ever-increasing consumption.

Recession and Financial, Impersonal Dictatorship

Modern culture has equated economic expansion with futurity, so that for the economists it is impossible to think the future independently of economic growth. But this identification has to be abandoned, and the concept of the future rethought. The mind of the economist cannot make the jump to this new dimension and cannot understand this paradigm shift. This is why the economy is a mess, and why economic wisdom cannot cope with the new reality. The financial semiotization of the economy is a war machine that destroys social resources and intellectual skills on a daily basis.

Look at what is happening in Europe. After centuries of industrial production, the European continent is rich. It has millions of technicians, poets, doctors, inventors, specialized factory workers, nuclear engineers… So how did we suddenly become so poor? Something very simple happened. The entirety of the wealth that workers have produced was poured into the strongboxes of a minuscule minority of exploiters and speculators. The whole mechanism of the European financial crisis is oriented toward the most extraordinary displacement of wealth that history has ever known, away from society and toward the financial class, toward financial capitalism.

The wealth produced by the collective intelligence has been drawn away and diverted. The effect of this displacement is the utter impoverishment of some of the richest places in the world, and the creation of a destructive financial machine that obliterates use-value and displaces monetary wealth.

Recession is the economist's way of semiotizing the present contradiction between the productive potency of the general intellect and current financial constraints.

Finance is an effect of the virtualization of reality, acting on the psycho-cognitive sphere of the economy. But at the same time, finance is an effect of the deterritorialization of wealth. It's not easy to identify financial capitalists as persons. Finance is not the monetary translation of a certain amount of physical goods; it is, rather, an effect of language.

Finance is the transversal function of immaterialization, and the performative action of indexicality. Statistics, figures, indexes, fears, and expectations are not linguistic representations of some economic referent that can be found somewhere in the physical world, signifiers referring to a signified. They are performing indexicals, acts of speech that produce immediate effects in the very instant of their enunciation.

This is why, when you go looking for the financial class, you cannot locate someone to talk to, or negotiate with, or an enemy to fight against. There are no enemies or people to negotiate with, but only mathematical implications, automatic social concatenations that you cannot dismantle or avoid.

Finance seems inhumane and pitiless because it is not human and therefore has no pity. It can be defined as a mathematical tumor traversing a large part of society. Those who are involved in the financial game are much more numerous than the property-owners of the old bourgeoisie. Often unwittingly and unwillingly, people have been dragged to invest their money and their futures in the financial game. Those who have invested their pensions in private funds, those who have signed mortgages semi-consciously, those who have fallen into the trap of quick credit have all become part of the traversal function of finance. They are poor people, workers, pensioners whose futures depend on the fluctuations of the stock market that they do not control at all, and that they do not even understand.

Future Exhaustion and Happy Frugality

Only if we're able to disentangle the future (the perception and conception of the future, and the very production of it) from the traps of growth and investment, will we find an escape from the vicious subjugation of life, wealth, and pleasure to the financial abstraction of semio-capital.

The key to this disentanglement may be found in a new form of wisdom which harmonizes with exhaustion. Exhaustion is a cursed word in the frame of modern culture, which is based on the cult of energy and the cult of male aggressivity. But energy is fading in the postmodern world, for many reasons that are easy to detect.

Energy is fading because of the demographic trend: mankind is growing old, as a whole, because of the prolongation of life expectancy, and because of the decreasing birth rate. A sense of exhaustion results from this process of general aging, and what has been considered a blessing— the prolonged life expectancy—may prove to be a misfortune, if the myth of energy is not restrained and replaced with a myth of solidarity and great compassion. Energy is also fading because basic physical resources like oil are doomed to extinction or dramatic reduction. Finally, energy is fading because competition is stupid in the age of the general intellect. The general intellect is not based on juvenile impetus and male aggressivity—on fighting, winning, and appropriation. It is based on cooperation and sharing.

This is why the future is over, and we are living in a space that is beyond the future. If we are able to come to terms with this postfuturistic condition, we'll renounce accumulation and growth, and will be happy in sharing the wealth from our past of industrial labor and from our present of collective intelligence.

If we are not able to do this, we will be doomed to a century of violence, misery, and war.

TIME, MONEY, AND LANGUAGE

Storing Time

Think about the following sentences:

> "Give me time."
> "You're wasting your time here."
> "I need more time."

These sentences are meaningless, as they presuppose that time is something than can be given or withdrawn, and imply that time is something that can be gained or lost, possessed and stored.

It is on this kind of absurdity that the economy is based, a technology aimed at the reification and the accumulation of time.

Timebank is a sort of tautology, because banks are essentially about time. What do you store in a bank? You store time. In a sense, you are storing your past, and you are also storing your future.

The essential transformation in the passage from modern bourgeois capitalism to contemporary semio-capitalism was a shift in the perception of the relation between money, language, and time.

This is my starting point: the relation between time, money, and language. I say that when you talk about banks, you're talking about storing time. But all the possible ways of storing and investing are each linked to changes in the history of capitalism, and also in the history of the relationship between capitalism and our life, subjectivity, and singularity.

It's quite difficult to be systematic about time, so I will not try to be systematic. I will try to find some reference points that may help us understand something about our present. What is happening in our present, from the point of view of time, language, and events? Well, let's have a look at the European landscape. You see how sad the European landscape is today.

I noticed that fact several days ago at the Berlin airport. I was there waiting for my flight, and I saw an old couple with smiling faces looking at the timetable, and also a young punk girl with tattoos. Everybody looked happy except me. I was the only sad person in the Berlin airport. I had my own personal reasons to be sad—that's not what I want to talk about. What is relevant here is that I am European and not German.

Take the Greeks, for instance. You know how sad they are, and also how desperate, and angry, too. But when you do not see any hope in your present situation, you're angry and desperate. And the Greeks are angry and desperate. And so are the Portuguese, not to mention the Irish. They were happy some years ago, and now, suddenly, they are in a different mood—as are all Europeans, except Germans.

Do you know why? Because German banks are full of our time. That's the problem. The German banks have stored Greek time, Portuguese time, Italian time, and Irish time, and now the German banks are asking for their money back. They have stored the futures of the Greeks, the Portuguese, the Italians, and so on. Debt is actually future time—a promise about the future. Greeks have been obliged to promise away their future time, and they have stored that promise in German banks.

Something is wrong with this exchange. You take my (future) time, and then want my money back. The crucial mystery, the crucial enigma, the crucial secret in the financial age of capitalism is precisely this: is the money that is stored in the bank my past time, (the time that I have spent in the past), or is it the money that ensures the possibility of my buying a future? Well, is it a secret or an enigma?

A secret is something that is hidden somewhere. You have to know the password, you have to find the right key, and then the secret will no longer be one. It will become a truth. An enigma is different, because you cannot find a key. The key is nowhere, and also the truth is nowhere. So, when we speak about financial capitalism, when we argue about the relation between time and future and debt, are we speaking of a secret, or are we speaking of an enigma?

I think we are speaking of an enigma, because nobody knows about the future, nobody knows what is hidden in the future time of debtors. So the only way to solve this enigma is with violence. Either you pay, or you are out. Either you give your present time as payment for the future time that you have stored in German banks, or you'll become poor. So in order to avoid being expelled from the European Union, the Greeks and the Portuguese and others are obliged to become poor. Recession, impoverishment, misery: this is the way we are paying for our (imaginary) future: debt.

Floating Values

You cannot find truth in financial capitalism, because the essential tool of financial capitalism is this: truth has disappeared, dissolved. It's no longer there. There is no more truth, only an exchange of signs, only a deterritorialization of meaning. In *Symbolic Exchange and Death*, a book published in 1976, Jean Baudrillard says that the whole system is falling into indeterminacy. This is the essential shift from industrial capitalism to semio-capitalism: indeterminacy takes the place of the fixed relation between labor-time and value, so that the whole regime of exchange falls into an aleatory system of floating values.

Financial capitalism is essentially based on the loss of relation between time and value.

In the first pages of *Capital*, Marx explains that value is time, the accumulation of time. Time objectified, time that has become things, goods, and value. But be careful: not just any kind of time is relevant in the determination of value, but the average social time that is needed to produce a certain good. If you are lazy, or too fast, that does not matter. What is important in the determination of value is the *average* time that is needed to produce a certain good. This was true in the good old days when it was possible to determine the time that was needed to produce something. Then things changed: all of a sudden, something new happened in the organization of work, and in production technology, in the relation between time, work, and value. Suddenly, work is no longer the physical, muscular work of industrial production. There are no longer material things, but signs; no longer the production of things which are tangible visible materials, but the production of something that is essentially semiotic.

When you want to establish the average time that is needed to produce a material object, you just have to do a simple calculation: how much physical labor time is needed to turn matter into that good. It's easy to state this, to decide how much time is needed to produce a material object. But try to decide how much time it takes to produce an idea. Try to decide how much time is necessary to produce a project, a style, an innovation. Well, you see that when the process of production becomes semiotic, the relationship between labor-time and value suddenly evaporates, dissolves into thin air. Baudrillard was the first thinker who understood and described this passage.

Baudrillard wrote *Symbolic Exchange and Death* in 1976. But some years before that, US President Richard Nixon did something that changed the world. The presidents of the US in those times were like prophets, not because they predicted the future zeitgeist, but because they were powerful enough to imprint their will, or the will of American capitalism, onto the future. And Nixon did something very, very important as far as changing the future went. Well, he decided to free the dollar from the gold standard.

He decided that the gold-standard system and the Bretton Woods system, based on a fixed relation between different currencies, was over. Since then, the dollar has been free from any fixed standard.

Independent, autonomous—or better, aleatory. Floating, undetermined.

Something aleatory is something that cannot be predicted, fixed, or determined in any way. Latin uses the word *ratio* in order to describe the fixed relationship, the standard, the measure. And in philosophical parlance, *ratio* refers to the universal standard of understanding things: reason.

After Nixon's decision, measurement ended. Standardization ended. The possibility of determining the average amount of time necessary to produce a good ended. Of course, that means that the United States of America, its president, Richard Nixon, decided that violence would take the place of measurement. In conditions of aleatority, what is the condition of the final decision? What is the action or process of determining value? Strength, force, violence. What is the final way of deciding something—for instance, deciding the exchange rate of the dollar? Violence, of course. Give me time.

The conjuncture between violence and the financialization of capitalism is not a casual and extemporaneous one. It's absolutely structural. There can be no financial economy without violence, because violence has now become the one single method of decision in the absence of the standard.

I will here pause in my elaboration of financial capitalism, but I want to come back to this subject at the end of this chapter. But first I want to say something now about time, forgetting, and the bank, if I can.

Fascism Femininity Futurism

We are accustomed—I say "we," meaning my generation, the last modern generation—we are accustomed to thinking about time in terms of progress, an endless process of growth, and also in terms of perfectibility.

The old, modern conception of futurity is crucial in understanding the way modernity has thought about time. The best definition of modern time you can find is in Marinetti's manifesto of 1909, "The Futurist Manifesto." Time is crucial to "The Futurist Manifesto." Even, when the futurists speak of despising "the woman," they are also speaking about time.

What is time in "The Futurist Manifesto"? The manifesto understands time as acceleration, and views acceleration as a process of increasing potency. This conception of acceleration is new in the history of thought and in the history of art. The idea that one's perception of time can be changed was already there in Impressionism and in Cézanne, but only in the sense of deceleration, in the sense of a becoming-slow of vision. Let's us not forget that Cézanne has a lot to do with Henri

Bergson, who translated the concept of time into the concept of duration. Bergson speaks of time in terms of perception, not extension. This is why Bergson is the philosopher who best interprets impressionist and symbolist poetics, as well as those of futurism. Because Bergson was offering a new perspective on time; he was speaking of time in terms of subjective duration, not in terms of the universal category of the human mind.

This is the crucial change from the classical age of bourgeois representation to the late-modern crisis and proliferation of viewpoints and streams of perception and consciousness.

The possibility of different intensities in temporal perception was introduced by Bergson and Cézanne, but especially by Marinetti and the Italian futurists.

While the Russian futurists were more interested in time from the point of view of their literary and artistic production but were less explicit in their poetics declarations, Italian futurists were trying to speak about time from the point of view of acceleration. And they said something that Paul Virilio has fully explained in his late-century books: velocity and acceleration are the modern tools of potency; industrial, political, and military potency are based on velocity in the late-modern age. Masculine potency is essentially perceived by Italian futurists as a problem of acceleration and we must not forget that Italian modernity was very concerned with the problem of the masculinization of perception: of time, of politics, of power.

One cannot understand Italian fascism if one doesn't start from the need for a defeminization of cultural self-perception. Italian fascism is based on despising the woman. Contempt for the woman is one of the crucial points of "The Futurist Manifesto," but it's also one of the crucial points of the creation of the ridiculous, miserable national pride of the Italians. Italians have always regarded themselves from a feminine perspective. The greatness of Italian culture is femininity, Mediterranean sweetness, taste for life, tenderness, and slowness. If you read Italian poetry—Dante, Petrarch, Torquato Tasso, Giacomo Leopardi, Ugo Foscolo— it always speaks of Italy as a beautiful woman, as a feminine body, sometimes a wounded or suffering one (Petrarch: *My Italy, though words cannot heal / The mortal wounds / So dense, I see on your lovely flesh…*), but also one with a feeling of pleasure and brightening. When being Italian was not shameful like it is today, Italy's self-identification was feminine.

Then something happened: nationalism, war, industrial competition arrived, and the main concern of Italian national culture became destroying this feminine self-perception, and affirming aggressivity and ludicrous masculinity: fascism is the turning point from feminine self-perception to masculine assertiveness. In the nineteenth century, Italian national culture became ashamed of the peaceful femininity of Mediterranean people, and began inoculating itself with testosterone. The result is a farcical show of aggressivity that is perfectly embodied by such murderous, cowardly clowns as Mussolini and Berlusconi.

When you speak of German fascism, it's not fake. It's not ridiculous, it's not funny. It's criminal, murderous, horrible, but not funny. But there is something that sounds false in Italian history. National pride, military aggressivity, industrial growth, and so on: all this is fake. This is why Italian fascism is often perceived as a farce, when unfortunately it was not. It was a farce, but a tragic and criminal farce, that provoked war, death, and devastation.

As far as time goes, Italian fascism was about forgetting laziness, slowness, and Mediterranean sensitivity, and affirming a different perception of time, one based on acceleration.

The feminine perception of Japanese identity is, in many ways, similar to the Italian one. And the modernization of the Meji restoration was based first of all on the defeminization of Japanese culture. Think, for instance, of the elimination of women in the environment of the emperor. From one day to the next, after 1870, women disappear and warriors appear, and the emperor has to become a true man. That kind of hysteria, the ridiculous, crazy, murderous hysteria of Italian and Japanese fascism, comes as a consequence of the denial and forced obliteration of the feminine side of those cultures.

Italian futurism is a good essential introduction to the twentieth century, because the twentieth century can be defined as the century that trusted in the future. Futurism asserted the idea that the future was the better dimension of time, not the past. When in fact, futurism is all about the destruction of the past, and the emphasis on and glorification of the future.

Now the glory of the future is over. We no longer trust the future, as the futurists—and the moderns, in general—did. What has happened?

1977

I want to focus on the crucial year 1977. I think that 1977 is especially important for many reasons. Don't forget that 1977 is the year when Charlie Chaplin dies. The death of that man, in my perception, represents the end of the possibility of a gentle modernity, the end of the perception of time as a contradictory, controversial place where different viewpoints can meet, conflict, and then find progressive agreement. Charlie Chaplin is the last man of modern times—the age of the machine, the horrible machine, coming into daily life and destroying daily life, but also the age of social conflict, of social consciousness, of solidarity. Charlie Chaplin is the man on the watch tower, looking at the city from a perilous vantage point, looking at the city of time, but also at the city where time can be negotiated and governed.

In 1977, Charlie Chaplin died. But I also want to remember that 1977 is the year when Steve Jobs and Steve Wozniak, in their small garage in Silicon Valley, created the user-friendly interfaces for the digital acceleration and mandatory unification of time. The Apple trademark was registered in 1977.

That same year, the Metropolitan Indians rioted in the streets of Rome and Bologna; and on the banks of the Thames in the Queen's Jubilee, a group of young British musicians for the first time cried *no future*. Don't think about your future. You don't have one. What Sid Vicious and the other Sex Pistols screamed and declared in 1977 was the final premonition of the end of modern times, the end of industrial capitalism, and the beginning of a new age, which is an age of total violence: financial globalization, deregulation, total competition, infinite war.

If capitalism wants to continue to exist in the history of mankind, then the history of mankind has to become a site of total violence, because only violence is decisive. Beginning in 1977, the word "competition" becomes the crucial term for economists. I don't know if economics can be considered a science. I don't think it can. I think it is a technology. It is a technology whose aim is the transformation of time into labor, and labor-time into value, and the transformation of our relation with nature into one of scarcity, need, and consumption.

But since 1977, the project of the science of economics (or technology, I don't know) is the submission of human relationships to one single goal: competition, competition, competition. Now "competition" has become a natural word, a normal word. This is not right, because "competition" means violence, war.

This is the meaning of competition. Otherwise, you forget the meaning of words. You forget that competition equals war. Deleuze and Guattari, in *A Thousand Plateaus*, try to define fascism, and they say: fascism is when a war machine is hidden in every niche, when in every nook and in every cranny of daily life a war machine is hidden. This is fascism.

So I would say that neoliberalism is the most perfect form of fascism, in terms of Deleuze and Guattari's definition. Competition is the concealment of a war machine in every niche of daily life: the kingdom of competition is fascism perfected.

Semio-inflation

I want to say something about semio-inflation, about the special kind of inflation that happens in the field of information, of understanding, of meaning, and of affection.

William Burroughs said that inflation is essentially when you need more money to buy less things. I say that semio-inflation is when you need more signs, words, and information to buy less meaning. It is a problem of acceleration. It is a kind of hyperfuturism when the old accelerative conception of the future is the crucial tool for the capitalist goat.

Karl Marx has already said something similar. When Marx speaks of productivity, and of relative surplus value, he's speaking about acceleration. He says that, if you want to obtain a growth in productivity, which is also a growth in surplus value, you need to accelerate work time. But at a certain point acceleration steps and jumps to another dimension, to what Baudrillard would call hyperacceleration.

The acceleration of productivity in the sphere of industrial production is about intensifying the rhythm of the machine so that workers are forced to move faster in manipulating physical matter and producing physical things. When the main tool of production begins to be cognitive labor, then acceleration enters another phase, another dimension. Increasing productivity in the sphere of semio-capitalism is essentially a problem of accelerating the infosphere.

In the sphere of semio-capital, if you want to increase productivity, what you have to do is accelerate the infosphere, the environment where information races toward the brain.

What happens, then, to our brain—to the social brain? Cognition takes time. Think of what attention is. Attention is the activation of physical reactions in the brain, and also of emotional, affective reactions. Attention cannot be infinitely accelerated. This is why the new economy has failed, at the end of the 1990s, after a long period of constant acceleration.

At the beginning of the last decade, in the year 2000, the dot-com crash was the consequence of an overexploitation of the social brain. After the explosion of the Internet bubble, suddenly several books about the attention economy appeared in bookstores.

All of a sudden, the economists became aware of the simple fact that the market of the semio-capitalist world is a market of attention. Market and attention had become the same thing. The crisis of 2000, the dot-com crash, was the effect of an overproduction in the field of attention.

Marx speaks of an overproduction crisis: if you produce too much of a certain good, people cannot buy all those things, and the goods will remain in the stores, unsold. So, the capitalist begins firing workers, because he does not need any more production, and this worsens the situation.

This is the overproduction crisis in the framework of industrial capitalism. What is the overproduction crisis when we enter the phase of semio-capital? The overproduction lies in the relation between the amount of semiotic goods produced by cognitive labor and the amount of time that is disposed of. A society's total quantity of attentive time is not boundless, because attention cannot be accelerated past a limit. One can accelerate one's attention; one can take amphetamines, for instance. We have techniques and drugs that give us the capability of being more productive in the field of attention. But we know the problem with that. You know how it ends. The 1990s were the dot-com era, the age of increasing productivity, increasing enthusiasm for production, increasing happiness of intellectual workers. But the 1990s were also the decade of Prozac mania. One cannot understand what Alan Greenspan calls "irrational exuberance" without taking into account the simple fact that millions of cognitive workers took tons of cocaine, amphetamine, and Prozac during the 1990s.

This can work for a time, and then it ends. All of a sudden, from one day to the next, after the excitement and the acceleration, comes the apocalypse.

Collapse

Do you remember the night of the turn of the century, when everybody was waiting for the Y2K bug? I was in front of my TV, waiting for the final collapse, and nothing happened. Nothing. It was the most horrible night of my life. I had staked all my credibility on promising everyone that that night would be the final one of our lives, and nothing happened at all, nothing. But there was an expectation of collapse in the air. How can we explain that expectation?

The collapse did not have to do with the millennium bug. The collapse represented the fall of the Prozac-fueled excitement in the social brain of the cognitive workers all over the world. When Alan Greenspan, in those months, said, "I feel an irrational exuberance in the markets," he was not speaking about the economy. He was speaking about the Prozac crash. He was speaking about the end of the cocaine high in the social brain of millions of cognitive workers.

What happened next? Well, the next step was an overproduction crisis in the field of semio-capitalism. In the first years of the century—2000, 2001—the problem was the perception of the coming collapse of capitalism, of the world economy. Then September 11th arrived, and overproduction became the solution to everything. Only a mad doctor would prescribe amphetamine to a depressed person, to a depressed organism. But that is exactly what happened after September 11th. The cognitive workers' organism, depressed for chemical and economic reasons, was submitted to the amphetaminic therapy of war by the mad doctor George Bush. The doctor was mad, and the result of this is now here: the infinite war.

Doctor Bush did not want to win the war. He was totally indifferent to winning or losing the war. It was so evident that starting a war in a place like Afghanistan, with an ally like Pakistan, is crazy, and a surefire way to lose. But the problem was not one of winning or losing: the problem concerned starting a war that would never end.

Infinite war is a sign of the kind of craziness that is a symptom of the inflation of meaning. More and more signs are buying less and less meaning.

What does one need when experiencing semio-inflation, when the infosphere starts moving faster and faster, and one's attention is unable to follow? What is needed is some sort of dispositive to make things easier, a dispositive to reduce the speed of the infosphere. It is a problem of time, acceleration, and deceleration: it is a problem of easification.

The end of modernity began with the collapse of the future, with Sid Vicious screaming *no future*. But postmodern history, as far as we have known, has been the history of a techno-linguistic machine which has increasingly penetrated every recess of daily life, every space of the social brain.

The techno-linguistic machine is giving language to human beings, and also taking the place of human beings in language for the current generation.

The first generation that learned more words from a machine than from their mothers has a problem concerning the relationship between words and the body, between words and affection. The separation of language learning from the body of the mother and from the body in general is changing language itself, and is changing the relation between language and the body. As far as we know, throughout human history access to language has always been mediated by trust in the mother's body. The relation between the signifier and the signified has always been guaranteed by the body of the mother, and therefore by the body of the other.

I know that water is "water" (actually, since I learned from my mother how to speak in Italian, I know that *acqua* is "acqua") because my mother, not a machine, told me "this is *acqua*." I know that the signifier points to the signified. My mother told me *acqua*, and I trust her body. What happens to the relation between language and desire when access to language is disconnected from the body?

When the relation between the signifier and the signified is no longer guaranteed by the presence of the body, my affective relation to the world starts to be disturbed. My relation to the world becomes functional, operational—faster, if you will, but precarious. This is the point where precariousness starts. At the point of disconnection between language and the body.

3

THE GENERAL INTELLECT IS LOOKING FOR A BODY

ABSTRACTION AND PATHOLOGY

Three Levels of Abstraction

In Marx's writings, abstraction is the main trend of capitalism, the general effect of capitalism on human activity. Marx means the abstraction of value from usefulness (use value), and the abstraction of productive work from concrete forms of human activity.

But in the sphere of semio-capitalism, two new levels of abstraction appear, as developments of the Marxian abstraction.

What does abstraction mean?

When Marx talks about abstract labor, he is referring to the separation of a worker's activity from concrete usefulness, which is what happens under capitalism. The use-value of the worker's product is only a step toward the real thing, which is value, which is surplus value. So the capitalist does not care

if his work is producing chickens or books or cars …
He cares only about this: how much value his work
can produce in a given unit of time. This is the
beginning of the process of capitalist abstraction.

In the late-modern phase of capitalism, digital
abstraction adds a second layer to capitalist
abstraction: transformation and production no
longer happen in the field of bodies, and material
manipulation, but in the field of interoperativity
between informational machines. Information
takes the place of things, and the body is cancelled
from the field of communication.

We then have a third level of abstraction, which
is financial abstraction. Finance means that the
process of valorization no longer passes through
the stage of use value, or even the production of
goods (physical or semiotic).

In the old industrial economy described by
Marx, the goal of production was already the
valorization of capital, through the extraction of
surplus value from labor. But in order to produce
value, the capitalist was still obliged to exchange
useful things; he was still obliged to produce cars
and books and bread.

When the referent is cancelled, when profit is
made possible by the mere circulation of money,
the production of cars, books, and bread become
superfluous. The accumulation of abstract value is
made possible through the subjection of human

beings to debt, and through predation on existing resources. The destruction of the real world starts from this emancipation of valorization from the production of useful things, and from the self-replication of value in the financial field. The emancipation of value from the referent leads to the destruction of the existing world. This is exactly what is happening under the cover of the so-called financial crisis, which is not a crisis at all.

In his book *Data Trash* (1994), Arthur Kroker and Michael A. Weinstein write that in the field of digital acceleration, more information means less meaning. In the sphere of the digital economy, the faster information circulates, the faster value is accumulated. But meaning slows down this process, as meaning needs time to be produced and to be elaborated and understood. So the acceleration of the info-flow implies an elimination of meaning.

In the sphere of the financial economy, the acceleration of financial circulation and valorization implies an elimination of the real world. The more you destroy physical things, physical resources, and the body, the more you can accelerate the circulation of financial flows.

In Greek, *parthenos* means virgin. Jesus Christ was created by parthenogenesis. The Virgin Mary gave birth to her son without any engagement in the reality of sex. The financial economy (like conceptual art) is a parthogenetic process. Actually, the monetization and financialization of the economy represent a parthogenization of the creation of value. Value does not emerge from a physical relationship between work and things, but rather from the self-replication of the parthogenetic force of finance.

As Maurizio Lazzarato points out in his book *The Making of the Indebted Man*, labor is no longer dominated by the physical force of power, but by the abstract force of finance: debt.

Digital abstraction leads to the virtualization of the physical act of meeting, and the manipulation of things. Financial abstraction leads to the separation of the circulation of money from the production process of value itself.

These new levels of abstraction not only concern the labor process—they encompass every space of social life. Digitalization and financialization have been transforming the very fabric of the social body, and inducing mutations.

The process of production is merging in the infosphere, and the acceleration of productivity is transforming into an acceleration of the information flows. Mental disorders and psychopathologies are symptoms of this dual process of virtual derealization and acceleration.

Digital abstraction, and the virtualization of social communication in general, has so deeply transformed the social environment that the cognitive processes of learning, speaking, imagining, and memorizing are affected.

In the sphere of neoliberal capitalism, because of the capture of feminine nervous and physical energies by the machinary of global exploitation, mothers are less and less the source of language: they are separated from the bodies of children by salaried labor, by the networked mobilization of their mental energies, and also by the globalization of the affective market. Millions of women leave their children in Manila and Nairobi and go to New York or London to look after the children of cognitive workers who leave their own children at home to go to offices.

Mothers are replaced by linguistic machines that are constantly talking and showing. The connective generation is learning language in a framework where the relation between language learning and the affective body tends to be less and less relevant.

What are the long-term effects of this separation of language from the mother's body? What are the long-term effects of the automation of language learning?

I have no final answers to these questions, and we cannot yet draw final conclusions about the self-consciousness of the first connective generation, which is now entering the scene of the world. The movements erupting in Europe and in the Arab world may be the first glimpses of a long-term process of self-organization by the precarious, connective generation around the world. Who knows what the future holds?

Over the last decade psychosocial research and the phenomenology of art, cinema, and novels has revealed a growing fragility of the affective relation, and an increase in mental pathologies: attention deficit disorders, depression, panic, and suicidal behavior have been rising in the collective experience of the new generation.

The literary and artistic phenomenology of the first decade of this century has told a story of creeping disease in the psychosphere. *The Corrections* by Jonathan Franzen, *Elephant* by Gus Van Sant, *Time* by Kim Ki Duk, *The Social Network* by David Fincher, *No One Belongs Here More Than You* by Miranda July, *We Have a Pope* by Nanni Moretti—to name just some of the books and films that seem to me to have grasped the innermost sentiment of the decade—all display a landscape of psychic breakdown.

In their book *Les passions tristes* (The sad passions), Miguel Benasayag and Gérard Schmit retrace their experience as psychoanalysts who have been working for many years in the *banlieux* of Paris among young people. In their account, the very perception of the future has changed among the young *banlieusards*, in that the future is no longer conceived as promise, but as a threat. The field of desire has been invaded by anxiogenous flows: the acceleration of the infosphere has expanded expectations, semiotic stimulation, and nervous excitement up to the point of collapse.

Desire and Money

Desire and money have a controversial relation. Money is about buying; desire is about creating. Deleuze and Guattari's decisive move, going back to their first collaboration, *Anti-Oedipus*, was to draw a conceptual distinction between desire and need. Desire should not be seen as a condition of scarcity, of *manque*; rather, it has to be seen as an enhancer of vision, as a creative activity.

When money takes the lead in the psychic investment of society—as in the aftermath of the neoliberal triumph—desire takes a paradoxical turn and starts to produce need, scarcity, and misery. The effect of financial abstraction is the constant deterritorialization of desire. In the traps of advertising and consumerism, desire is dragged into a relation of dependence with the financial machine. In the 1990s, the credit card system invested American desire, opening the way to the deception of boundless consumption. The economic investment of desire was the original fount of the virtual economy in the 1990s, and then the explosion of the dot-com bubble in

2000 precipitated a short-circuiting of desire into panic and depression.

Since September 2008, Americans have been suffering the backlash: unemployment, urban misery, social spending cuts, infrastructure decay.

The financial ideology is thriving in the context of social precariousness. When the prospects are uncertain, you are invited to bet on the future. Lottery, net trading, risk-taking—these are the opportunities financial capitalism is offering everybody. Bubbles grow, then bust, and the vast majority of people lose their money. You can use your credit card to its limit and beyond, betting on future revenues that will not arrive. You are debtor to a bank that is thriving thanks to your being deceived. Transforming desire into need, the financial investment of desire paves the way to dependency and misery.

The modern bourgeoisie was a strongly territorialized class, linked to material assets; they were a class acutely conscious of their relation with territory and community. Their wealth and prosperity were based on the ownership of physical assets: factories, houses, goods stored in warehouses. The well-being of workers was essential to the creation of a mass market and the thriving of bourgeois capitalism.

The industrial bourgeoisie exploited workers with the goal of developing society, and developed society in order to extract surplus value from workers. The revenue of the financial class, on the contrary, is not linked to the actual enrichment of the territory, of the city, of the *bourg*. When the *bourg* goes global, the bourgeoisie disappears, and bourgeois morality dissolves. The bourgeois unconscious was based on the separation of work and desire, on repression of the sexual drive and postponement of pleasure.

At the end of the bourgeois era, in the aftermath of financial capitalism's triumph, desire invades the space of the market, and the market invades the space of desire. Work and self-realization have to merge in the new economic vision: individuals have to become free agents. There is no longer a distinction between life time and work time: all of your time has to be devoted to earning money, as money has taken the place of desire.

As the Italian psychoanalyst Massimo Recalcati has pointed out in *L'uomo senza inconscio* (Man without unconscious; 2010), in the finanical era the social unconscious explodes, as it is everywhere. Deterritorialization becomes the perpetual condition of money and of desire.

The financial class that dominates the contemporary scene has neither attachments to territory nor to material production, because its power and wealth are founded on the total abstraction of a digitally multiplied finance. This digital-financial hyperabstraction is liquidating both the living body of the planet and the social body.

One of the most important effects of the Internet in the economy has been the diffusion of online trading among young professionals and cognitive workers: this countless proliferation of investors ensures the impossibity of finding a relationship between personal responsibility and the social effects of an investment. More and more often, the economic stake of a financial investment is negative, destructive of concrete resources. You can bet on the closure of a factory, the firing of workers, the death of people; you can bet on the spread of a disease. The financial economy can act, and is acting more and more, as a counter-productive force, as the accumulation of money is becoming completely abstracted from the actual creation of use-value.

When the dot-com economy crashed in the first months of 2000, many thought that the virtual world was doomed to decay. Actually, things have turned out differently: the nonexistent world evoked by digital technology has not dissolved, the Internet is here to stay, and the virtualization of social communication did not stop in 2000.

But in 2000, the dot-com crash marked an irreversible turn in the social relation between financial capital and cognitive work. Cognitarians, who had been able to create enterprise, were disowned and separated from financial power, and finally consigned to the role of a precarious work force.

The digital mobilization of desire, the acceleration of the infosphere, the overloading of collective attention, and an overuse of psychopharmaceutical stimulants were the psychic triggers of the dot-com/Prozac crash, and that crash opened the door to the disempowerment of cognitive labor. The dismantling of the general intellect began in the agonies of the dot-com Prozac crash. The euphoric decade of Clinton's imperial illusion gave way to a decade of infinite war, global terror, and suicide. The financial collapse of 2008 is the predictable conclusion of this age of financial *Ersatz*, but the financial class does not want to recognize the failure, and a dangerous doubling-down on neoliberal monetarist policies is being enforced everywhere around the world.

The ideology that fostered the Internet in the 1990s was based on a premise of infinite energy, infinite expansion, infinite resources. The old economy—the economy of the old industrial times—was based on a premise of scarcity, as it was based on material resources that could be exhausted. The new economy, instead, was envisioned as a long, unending boom by Peter Schwartz and Peter Leyden, the *Wired* ideologues. This idea was based on the premise of the infinite potency of the net.

Because the net is an ever-expanding sphere of immaterial substance (information), because intellectual productivity is not limited by material constraints, the networked economy was expected to last forever and to provoke an everlasting expansion of market and value.

Only one of these premises was true: the net actually is an ever-expanding space, but the infinity of mental energy was an illusion. The wired ideology has proven false because the ideologues did not consider the limits of the subjective side of the economy. The attention market went into overload, resulting in a semiotic overproduction. And the global mind went crazy because individual brains and individual bodies are not capable of limitlessly going faster and faster and faster. The exhaustibility of psychic resources is the intrinsic limit of the cybersphere. The dream of the networked economy's endless boom broke because psychic energy is not boundless, because the physical resources of the planet are not boundless, and because the infinite potency of the networked collective intelligence is limited by the finitude of psychic energy.

IMPOSSIBLE FRIENDSHIP
(The Logic of *Ersatz* in Fincher's Facebook Movie)

Financial capitalism and precarious work, loneliness, suffering, and the atrophy of empathy and sensibility: this is the subject of David Fincher's excellent movie, *The Social Network*. The story is about the creation and early diffusion of the social network Facebook, about one enterprise in the age of financial semio-capitalism. But the focus of the movie shifts to the psychological side of the evolution of the Internet, in the context of the info-acceleration and stimulus-intensification that broadband technology has made possible. Love, friendship, affection—the whole sphere of emotionality is invested by the intensification of the rhythm of the infosphere.

Although the narrative concerns the beginnings of Facebook, and the ensuing legal conflicts and trials correspond to the real story, biographical details in the film (for instance, the end of a love affair in the first scene of the movie) are not necessarily factual, but are useful for a full understanding of the affective side of the social life of the cognitarian labor force.

The main character of the film, Mark Zuckerberg, may obviously be described as a winner: he is the youngest billionaire in the world, and he owns a company that in only a few years has become well-known worldwide with five-hundred million subscribers. Nonetheless, it is difficult to see him as a happy person, and he can be described as a loser if you consider his relationships with women and colleagues. Friendship seems impossible for him, and the success of his website is granted by the artificial substitution (*Ersatz*) of friendship and love with standardized protocols. Existential unhappiness and commercial success can be viewed as two sides of the same coin: Fincher's movie very skillfully interprets the psychological needs of Zuckerberg's generation by portraying loneliness and affective frustration as his intimate psycho-scape.

Desire is diverted from physical contact and invested in the abstract field of simulated seduction, in the infinite space of the image. The boundless enhancement of disembodied imagination leads to the virtualization of erotic experience, infinite flight from one object to the next. Value, money, financial excitement: these are the perfect forms of this virtualization of desire. The permanent mobilization of psychic energy in the economic sphere is simultaneously the cause and the effect of the virtualization of contact. The very word "contact" comes to mean the exact opposite of contact: not bodily touch, not epidermic perception of the sensuous presence of the other, but purely intellectual intentionality, virtual cognizability of the other. It is hard to predict what sort of long-term mutation is underway in human evolution. As far as we know, this virtual investment of desire is currently provoking a pathogenic fragilization of social solidarity and a stiffening of empathic feeling.

The genius of Zuckerberg essentially consists in his ability to exploit the suffering of the crowd, the miserable energies of collective loneliness and frustration. The original idea for the website came from two rich Harvard twins named Tyler and Cameron Winklevoss, who wanted to hire Zuckerberg as a programmer. Zuckerberg pretends to work for them, but actually takes hold of their idea, although he is much more capable than they are in terms of linking the project to the psychic needs arising from contemporary alienation.

Did Zuckerberg steal the idea from these two undergraduates? Yes and no. Actually, in the network it's impossible to clearly distinguish the different moments of the valorization process, because the productive force of the net is collective, while profits are private. Here we find the irremediable contradiction between the collective intelligence of the net and the private appropriation of its products, shaking the very foundation of semio-capitalism.

The movie presents an interesting perspective on life and work in the age of precarity. The word "precarious" means aleatory, uncertain, unstable, and it refers not only to the uncertainty of the labor relation, but also to the fragmentation of time and the unceasing deterritorialization of the factors of social production. Both labor and capital, in fact, no longer have a stable relation to territory or community. Capital flows in the financial circuits, and enterprise is no longer based on territorialized material assets, but on signs, ideas, information, knowledge, and linguistic exchange. Enterprise is no longer linked to territory and the work process is no longer based on a community of workers, living together in a factory day after day, but instead takes the form of an ever-changing recombination of time fragments connected in the global network. Cognitive workers do not meet in the same place every day, but remain alone in their networked cubicles, where they answer to the requests of ever-changing employers. The capitalist no longer signs agreements in order to exploit the productive energies of the worker during his overall working life. He no longer purchases the entire availability of the worker. He hires a fragment of available time, a fractal, compatible with the protocols of interfunctionality, and recombinable with other fragments of time.

Industrial workers experienced solidarity because they met each other every day and were members of the same living community who shared the same interests, while the Internet worker is alone and unable to create solidarity because everybody is obliged to compete in the labor market and in the daily fight for a precarious salary. Loneliness and lack of human solidarity not only characterize the situation of the worker, but also that of the entrepreneur. The border separating labor and enterprise is confused in the sphere of cognitive work. Although Mark Zuckerberg is a billionaire, the way he spends his work day is not dissimilar to the way his employees spend theirs. They all sit in front of computers and type on keyboards.

The main character of the movie—the Zuckerberg portrayed by Fincher—has only one friend: Edouard Severin, who becomes the financer of the initial Facebook enterprise. When the growth of the enterprise demands new financers, Zuckerberg does not hesitate to betray his only friend.

This is not only characteristic of personal relations in the financial world, but is unfortunately also characteristic of relations between workers. Although the movie portrays a billionaire, it also tells the story of the social condition of labor: the impossibility of friendship in the present condition of the virtual abstraction of sociality, and the impossibility of building solidarity in a society that turns life into an abstract container of competing fragments of time.

RESPIRATION, CONSPIRACY, AND SOLIDARITY

Once upon a time, I happened to take part in an action of the Living Theater. In an old Italian theater, some hundred people met for a collective mantra: an emission of harmonic sounds, shared breathing, and shared sound which lasts in time thanks to a vocal wave which goes from one mouth to the next, from one body to the next. I want to elaborate on the mantra as a form of composing the insurgent movement.

Let's consider the social relation from the point of view of harmony and disharmony among breathing singularities. Organisms meet, conflict, interact in common space. The wisdom of the Hindu yogin conceives of individual breathing (*atman*) as a relation of the organism with cosmic breath (*prana*) and the physical surrounding environment.

Physical organisms interact with the natural environment, with the city, the factory, the air. Psychic organisms also interact with the infosphere, the environment where info-stimulae circulate, influencing psychic reactions.

In late-modern times, we experience a growing pollution of air, water, and food. Industrial fall out is provoking an increase in asthma, lung cancer, and respiratory diseases. But there is another kind of pollution which concerns the psychic breathing of individual and collective organisms. Semiotic flows which are spread in the infosphere by the media system are polluting the psychosphere and provoking disharmony in the breathing of singularities: fear, anxiety, panic, and depression are the pathological symptoms of this kind of pollution.

Let's understand how singularities are linking in the social-psychic becoming. Concatenations between conscious and sensitive organisms can happen as conjunctive concatenations and also as connective concatenations. Human beings conjoin thanks to their ability to linguistically and sensuously interact. The phenomenon of linguistic communication has been widely studied by scholars, and we know that the media can modify and enrich it, but also impoverish it.

There is another level of the concatenation, sensibility, which should be better understood. Sensibility is the ability of the human being to communicate what cannot be said with words. Being available to conjunction, the social organism is open to affections, sensuous comprehension, and social solidarity. Cultural flows—music and poetry, as well as psychotropic substances—can favor, or obstruct and pollute, conjunctive ability.

Sensibility is also the faculty that allows us to enter into relation with entities not composed of our matter, not speaking our language, and not reducible to the communication of discreet, verbal, or digital signs.

Sensibility is the ability to harmonize with the rhizome.

Principles of connection and heterogeneity: any point of a rhizome can be connected to anything other, and must be. [...] *Collective assemblages of enunciation* function directly within *machinic assemblages*; it is not impossible to make a radical break between regimes of signs and their objects. [...] The orchid deterritorializes by forming an image, a tracing of a wasp; but the wasp reterritorializes on that image. The wasp is nevertheless deterritorialized, becoming a piece in the orchid's reproductive apparatus. But it reterritorializes the orchid by transporting its pollen. Wasp and orchid, as heterogeneous elements, form a rhizome. (Deleuze and Guattari 1987, 7–10)

On the ontological, teleological, or even the physical plane, the wasp and the orchid are not homogeneous. They even belong to two different natural realms. But this does not prevent them from working together in the sense of becoming a concatenation (*s'agencer*), and in so doing generating something that was not there before. "Be, Be, Be!" is the metaphysical scream that dominates hierarchical thought. Rhizomatic thought replies: "Concatenate, Concatenate, Concatenate!"

The principle of becoming lies in conjunctive concatenation:

... a becoming-wasp of the orchid and a becoming-orchid of the wasp. Each of these becomings brings about the deterritorialization of one term and the reterritorialization of the other; the two becomings interlink and form relays in a circulation of intensities pushing the deterritorialization ever further. There is neither imitation nor resemblance, only an exploding of two heterogeneous series on the line of flight composed by a common rhizome that can no longer be attributed to or subjugated by anything signifying. Rémy Chauvin expresses it well: "the *aparallel evolution* of two beings that have absolutely nothing to do with each other." (Deleuze and Guattari 1987, 10)

Conjunction/Connection

Conjunction and connection are two different modalities of social concatenation. Whilst conjunction means becoming-other, living, and the unpredictable concatenation of bodies, connection means the functional interoperability of organisms previously reduced to compatible linguistic units.

The spreading of the connective modality in social life (the network) creates the condition of an anthropological shift that we cannot yet fully understand. This shift involves a mutation of the conscious organism: in order to make the conscious organism compatible with the connective machine, its cognitive system has to be reformatted. Conscious and sensitive organisms are thus being subjected to a process of mutation that involves the faculties of attention, processing, decision, and expression. Info-flows have to be accelerated, and connective capacity has to be empowered, in order to comply with the recombinant technology of the global net.

In order to understand the present anthropological shift, we should focus on the meaning of conjunction and connection.

Conjunction is a becoming-other. In contrast, with connection each element remains distinct and interacts only functionally. Singularities change when they conjoin, they become something other than what they were before their conjunction. Love changes the lover and the combination of asignifying signs gives rise to the emergence of a previously nonexistent meaning.

Rather than a fusion of segments, connection entails a simple effect of machinic functionality. The functionality of the materials that connect is implicit in the connection as a functional modeling that prepares them for interfacing and interoperability. In order for connection to be possible, segments must be linguistically compatible. Connection requires a prior process whereby the elements that need to connect are made compatible. Indeed, the digital web extends through the progressive reduction of an increasing number of elements to a format, a standard, and a code that makes compatible different elements.

The process of change underway in our time is centered on the shift from conjunction to connection as the paradigm of exchange between conscious organisms. The leading factor of this change is the insertion of the electronic in the organic—the proliferation of artificial devices in the organic universe, the body, communication, and society. But the effect of this change is a transformation of the relationship between consciousness and sensibility, and an increasing desensitization in the exchange of signs.

Conjunction is the meeting and fusion of round and irregular shapes that are continuously weaseling their way about without precision, repetition, or perfection. Connection is the punctual and repeatable interaction of algorithmic functions, straight lines, and points that overlap perfectly, and plug in or out according to discrete modes of interaction that render the different parts compatible to a preestablished standard. The shift from conjunction to connection as the predominant mode of interaction of conscious organisms is a consequence of the gradual digitalization of signs and the increasing mediatization of relations.

The digitalization of communicative processes induces a sort of desensitization to the curve, the continuous process of gradual becoming; and a sort of sensitization to the code, sudden changes of state, and series of discrete signs.

Conjunction entails a semantic criterion of interpretation. The other, who enters in conjunction with you, sends signs whose meanings you must interpret, by tracing if necessary the intention, the context, the shade, the unsaid.

Connection requires a criterion of interpretation that is purely syntactic. The interpreter must recognize a sequence and be able to carry out the operation foreseen by the "general syntax" (or operating system); there can be no margins for ambiguity in the exchange of messages, nor can the intention be manifest though nuances. The gradual translation of semantic differences into syntactic differences is the process that led from modern scientific rationalism to cybernetics, and eventually made the creation of a digital web possible.

But if you extend the syntactic method of interpretation to human beings, a cognitive and psychic mutation is underway.

This mutation is actually producing painful effects on the conscious organism, and these effects can be interpreted with the categories of psychopathology: dyslexia, anxiety and apathy, panic and depression. However, pathological description does not grasp the deep meaning of the question. What is more important, in fact, is the conscious organism's attempt to adapt to a changing environment.

In order to efficiently interact with the connective environment, the conscious and sensitive organism starts to suppress to a certain degree what we call sensibility. This is, in my opinion, the core of the cognitive reformatting that is underway.

Sensibility—i.e., the ability to interpret and understand what cannot be expressed in verbal or digital signs—can be useless and also dangerous in an integrated system of connective nature. Sensibility slows interpretation procedures, making decodification aleatory, ambiguous, and uncertain, and thus reducing the competitive efficiency of the semiotic agent.

The ethical dimension is involved in this process: a sort of ethical insensibility seems to mark the behavior of the humans of the last generation. But if we want to understand the disturbance in the ethical sphere, we should displace our attention toward the aesthetic field. The ethical disorder, the inability to ethically manage individual and collective life, seems to follow from a disturbance of the aesthesia, the perception of the other and of the self.

Composition and Recombination

When I say composition, I mean a form of shared respiration: cospiration, conspiracy, growing together, conjoined expectations, coalescing lifestyles.

When I say recombination, I mean compatibility and functional operativity.

When the relation between social components (individuals) is predominantly recombinant, the social organism stiffens and gets frail: solidarity becomes difficult.

Social solidarity is not an ethical or ideological value: it depends on the continuousness of the relation between individuals in time and in space. The material foundation of solidarity is the perception of the continuity of the body in the body, and the immediate understanding of the consistency of my interest and your interest.

The communist conspiracy, for instance, was the psychic and cultural energy that made solidarity possible inside the social body of the industrial worker class, notwithstanding the authoritarian reality of communist realizations.

Since the 1980s, precarity has provoked a process of desolidarization and disaggregation of the social composition of work. Virtualization has been a complementary cause of desolidarization: precarization makes the social body frail at the level of work, while virtualization makes the social body frail at the level of affection.

Inside the precarious conditions of labor, collective breath is fragmented, submitted to the accelerating rhythms of the virtual machine: the fractal fragmentation of labor is parallel and complementary to the fractalization of financial capital. Financial capitalism is deterritorialized and virtual, and acts as a constant recombination of virtual fragments of abstract ownership.

Because of the introduction of the connective principle in social communication, the ability to sympathize weakens, and functional recombination happens on impersonal ground.

Disempathy is the consequence of this disharmonization of social communication. The sexuality of the fractal body is exposed in the form of panic, and desire is driven simultaneously in countless directions, in the frigid orgy of pornography.

Rhythm and Refrain

Late-modern rhythm has been scanned by the ordered noise of the machine. Rock and punk music have inherited the knack for mechanical rhythm, although in the end they turn this gift into rage against the machine. In his book *Sonic Warfare: Sound, Affect, and the Ecology of Fear* (2010), Steve Goodman describes the rhythmic aggression against social life:

> From Hitler's use of the loudspeaker as a mechanism for affective mobilization during World War II, through to Bin Laden's audio-taped messages, the techniques of sonic warfare have now percolated into the everyday. (Goodman 2002, 5)

In order to describe the relation between the surrounding soundscape and the traces of singularity, Guattari speaks of *ritournelle*, or refrain.

A child singing in the night because it is afraid of the dark seeks to regain control of events that deterritorialized too quickly for her liking and started to proliferate on the side of the cosmos and the Imaginary. Every individual, every group, every nation is thus "equipped" with a basic range of incantatory refrains. (Guattari 2011, 107)

The refrain is an obsessive ritual that allows the individual—the conscious organism in continuous variation—to find identification points, and to territorialize herself and to represent herself in relation to the surrounding world. The refrain is the modality of semiotization that allows an individual (a group, a people, a nation, a subculture, a movement) to receive and project the world according to reproducible and communicable formats.

In order for the cosmic, social, and molecular universe to be filtered through individual perception, semiotic filters must act, and we call them refrains.

The perception of time by a society is shaped by social refrains.

From this perspective, universal time appears to be no more than a hypothetical projection, a time of generalized equivalence, a "flattened" capitalistic time. (Guattari 1995, 16)

The main cultural transformation of modern capitalism has been the creation of refrains of temporal perception that pervade and discipline society: the refrain of factory work, the refrain of salary, the refrain of the assembly line.

The digital transition has brought along with it new refrains: electronic fragmentation, information overload, acceleration of the semiotic exchange, fractalization of time, competition.

The essential feature of refrain is rhythm, and rhythm is a special configuration of the relation between singular refrain and universal chaos.

> Chaos is not the opposite of rhythm, but the milieu of all milieus. There is rhythm whenever there is a transcoded passage from one milieu to another, a communication of milieus, coordination between heterogeneous space-times. (Deleuze and Guattari 1987, 345)

Rhythm is the relation of a subjective flow of signs (musical, poetic, gestual signs) with the environment: the cosmic environment, earthly environment, social environment.

Rhythm is everywhere in social life. Work, war, rituals, and social movements each have their special rhythm.

At the chaosmotic level, rhythm is the concatenation between breathing and the surrounding universe. In Guattari's parlance, refrain is the only way of creating this concatenation, this *agencement* between singularity and environment.

At the social level, rhythm is the relation between the body and the social concatenation of language.

The social environment is marked by refrains, repetitions of gestures and signs that simultaneously express the singular mode and the relation between the agency and the environment.

Mantra

The uprising against financial capitalism that began in the European countries in 2011 can be seen as a mantra, as an attempt to reactivate the conjunctive body, as a form of therapy on the disempathetic pathologies crossing the social skin and social soul.

Upheaval, uprising, insurrection, and riots: these words should not be used in a militaristic sense. The organization of violent actions by the anti-capitalist movement would not be smart, as violence is a pathological demonstration of impotence when power is protected by armies of professional killers. Nevertheless, we'll be witness to massive explosions of precarious rage and violence, as in England in August 2011, as in Rome on October 15th.

The uprising will frequently give way to phenomena of psychopathic violence. These should not surprise us; we should not condemn these acts as criminal. For too long has financial dictatorship compressed the social body, and the cynicism of the ruling class has become repugnant.

The uprising is a therapy for this kind of psychopathology.

The uprising is not a form of judgment, but a form of healing.

And this healing is made possible by a mantra that rises, stronger and stronger, as solidarity resurfaces in daily life.

It is useless to preach a sermon to those who can only express their revolt in a violent way. The medic does not judge, but heals, and the task of the movement is to act as a medic, not as a judge.

What we should be able to communicate to the rioters, the looters, the black bloc, and the *casseurs* is a truth that we have to build together and to spread: that a collective mantra chanted by millions of people will tear down the walls of Jericho much better than a pickaxe or a bomb.

4

POETRY AND FINANCE

EMANCIPATION OF THE SIGN: POETRY AND FINANCE IN THE TWENTIETH CENTURY

Money and language have something in common: they are nothing and they move everything. They are nothing but symbols, conventions, *flatus vocis*, but they have the power of persuading human beings to act, to work, to transform physical things.

> Money makes things happen. It is the source of action in the world and perhaps the only power we invest in. Perhaps in every other respect, in every other value, bankruptcy has been declared, giving money the power of some sacred deity, demanding to be recognized. Economics no longer persuades money to behave. Numbers cannot make the beast lie down and be quiet or sit up and do tricks. Thus, as we suspected all along, economics falsely imitates science. At best, economics is a neurosis of money, a symptom

contrived to hold the beast in abeyance [...]
Thus economics shares the language of psychopathology, inflation, depression, lows and heights, slumps and peaks, investments and losses, and the economy remains caught in manipulations of acting stimulated or depressed, drawing attention to itself, egotistically unaware of its own soul. Economists, brokers, accountants, financiers, all assisted by lawyers, are the priests of the cult of money, reciting their prayers to make the power of money work without imagination. (Sardello 1983, 1–2)

Financial capitalism is based on the autonomization of the dynamics of money, but more deeply on the autonomization of value production from the physical interaction of things.

The passage from the industrial abstraction of work to the digital abstraction of world implies an immaterialization of the labor process.

Jean Baudrillard has proposed a general semiology of simulation based on the premise of the end of referentiality, in the economic as well as in the linguistic field. In *The Mirror of Production*, Baudrillard writes: "need, use value, and the referent 'do not exist.' They are only concepts produced and projected into a generic dimension by the development of the very system of exchange value." (Baudrillard 1975, 30)

The process of the autonomization of money is a particular level of this general trend, but it also has a long history, according to Marc Shell in *Money, Language, and Thought*.

Between the electrum money of ancient Lydia and the electric money of contemporary America there occurred a historically momentous change. The exchange value of the earliest coins derived wholly from the material substance (electrum) of the ingots of which the coins were made and not from the inscriptions stamped into these ingots. The eventual development of coins whose politically authorized inscriptions were inadequate to the weights and purities of the ingots into which the inscriptions were stamped precipitated awareness of quandries about the relationship between face value (intellectual currency) and substantial value (material currency). This difference between inscription and thing grew greater with the introduction of paper moneys. Paper, the material substance on which the inscriptions were printed, was supposed to make no difference in exchange, and metal or electrum, the material substance to which the inscriptions referred, was connected with those inscriptions in increasingly abstract ways. With the advent of electronic fund-transfers the link between inscription and substance was broken. The matter of electric money does not matter. (Shell 1982, 1)

As I've already said, the dephysicalization of money is part of the general process of abstraction which is the all-encompassing tendency of capitalism.

Marx's theory of value is based on the concept of abstract work: because it is the source and the measure of value, work has to sever its relation to the concrete usefulness of its activity and product. Concrete usefulness does not matter from the point of view of valorization. Baudrillard speaks of the relation between signification and language in the same vein. The abstraction process at the core of the capitalist capture (subsumption) of work implies abstraction from the need for the concreteness of products: the referent is erased.

> The rational, referential, historical and functional machines of consciousness correspond to industrial machines. The aleatory, nonreferential, transferential, indeterminate and floating machines of the unconscious respond to the aleatory machines of the code [...] The systemic strategy is merely to invoke a number of floating values in this hyperreality. This is true of the unconscious as it is of money and theories. Value rules according to the indiscernible order of generation by means of

models, according to the infinite chains of simulation. (Baudrillard 1993, 3)

The crucial point of Baudrillard's critique is that referentiality and the (in)determination of value has come to an end. In the sphere of the market, things are not considered from the point of view of their concrete usefulness, but from that of their exchangeability and exchange value. Similarly, in the sphere of communication, language is traded and valued as something that is performed. Effectiveness, not truth value, is the rule of language in the sphere of communication. Pragmatics, not hermeneutics, is the methodology for understanding social communication, particularly in the age of new media.

Retracing the process of dereferentialization in both semiotics and economics, Baudrillard speaks of the emancipation of the sign.

A revolution has put an end to this "classical" economics of value, a revolution of value itself, which carries value beyond its commodity form into its radical form.

This revolution consists in the dislocation of the two aspects of the law of value, which were thought to be coherent and eternally bound as if by a natural law. *Referential value is annihilated, giving the structural play of value the upper hand.*

The structural dimension becomes autonomous by excluding the referential dimension, and is instituted upon the death of reference [...] from now on, signs are exchanged against each other rather than against the real (it is not that they just happen to be exchanged with each other, they do so *on condition* that they are no longer exchanged against the real). The emancipation of the sign. (Baudrillard,1993, 6–7)

The emancipation of the sign from the referential function may be seen as the general trend of late Modernity, the prevailing tendency in literature and art as in science and in politics.

In the following pages I want to retrace the evolution of poetry in the passage from romantic realism to symbolist transrealism.

Symbolism opened a new space for poetic praxis, starting from the emancipation of the word from its referential task.

The emancipation of money—the financial sign—from the industrial production of things follows the same semiotic procedure, from referential to nonreferential signification.

But the analogy between economy and language should not mislead us: although money and language have something in common, their destinies do not coincide, as language exceeds economic exchange. Poetry is the language of nonexchangeability, the return of infinite hermeneutics, and the return of the sensuous body of language.

I'm talking about poetry here as an excess of language, a hidden resource which enables us to shift from one paradigm to another.

A PLACE WE DO NOT KNOW

> Angel, if there were a place we do not know, and there
> On some ineffable carpet, the lovers, who never
> Could achieve fulfillment here, could show
> Their bold lofty figures of heart-swings,
> Their towers of ecstasy, their pyramid
> That long since, where there was no standing-ground,
> Were tremblingly propped together—could succeed
> Before the spectators around them, the innumerable
>   silent dead:
> Would not these then throw their last, ever-hoarded,
> Ever-hidden, unknown to us, eternally
> Valid coins of happiness
> Before their pair with the finally genuine smile
> On the assuaged carpet?
> —Rainer Maria Rilke, "Fifth Elegy"
>   (Translated by C.F. MacIntyre)

The reactivation of the social body is the precondition for the full deployment of the general intellect.

Since 2001 we have witnessed a dismantling of the general intellect that started after the dot-com crash in the spring of 2000. During the first decade of the new century, cognitive labor was disempowered and subjected to precarization.

The social and affective body of the cognitive workers has been separated from their daily activity of production. The new alienation is based on this separation, on the virtualization of social relations. The new alienation takes the form of psychic suffering, panic, depression, and a suicidal tide. This is the affective character of the first generation of people who have learned more words from a machine than from the mother.

The insurrection against financial capitalism is aimed to recompose the social and affective body. The student struggles that have exploded in Europe since the fall of 2010 should not be seen as sudden outbursts of rage, but as the beginnings of a long-lasting process that will encompass the next decade: a cognitarian insurrection of sorts. Insurrection means a rising up, and also implies the full deployment of the potencies of the actor. The actor that is appearing on the historical scene today is the general intellect in its process of subjectivation. The potencies of this actor are the potencies of collective intelligence in the network, the potencies of knowledge, reduced to the narrow dogmatic utilization that the capitalist economy is forcing on them.

The full deployment of the general intellect falls beyond the sphere of capitalism.

When general intellect will be able to reconstitute its social and erotic body, capitalist rule will become obsolete. This is the new consciousness that comes from the explosion of the last months of 2010, from the reclamation of knowledge's autonomy.

In the same period of the student revolt, the Wikileaks event has exposed the other face of cognitarian subjectivation. What is its meaning, beyond the remarkable effect that Wikileaks has had in the field of diplomacy and politics and war, and obviously in the field of information?

Wikileaks has displayed the infinite potency of the collective networked intelligence. The unleashing of the creative force of the general intellect is the momentous event that Julian Assange has been able to orchestrate. I don't think that we really needed to know the contents of all those cables and e-mails that Wikileaks disclosed. Actually, we already knew that diplomats are paid to lie, and that soldiers are paid for killing civilians.

Many interesting things have come out from the disclosures, but this is not my focus here. What is more important concerning this event is the activation of solidarity, complicity, and independent collaboration between cognitarians that it represents: between programmers, hardware technicians, journalists, and artists who all take part in an informational process. The activation of the potency of this connected intelligence, autonomously from its capitalist use, is the lesson Wikileaks has to offer. And the new generation of rebels will find in this lesson a way to the autonomization and self-organization of the general intellect.

In street demonstrations, the social and erotic body of the cognitarians is finding rhythm and empathy. The main stake of street actions is the reactivation of the body of the general intellect. Bodily sensibility, blurred and stressed by precarity and competition, are finding new modes of expression, so that desire may begin flowing again.

Connection and Sensibility

Sensibility is the ability to understand what cannot be verbalized, and it has been a victim of the precarization and fractalization of time. In order to reactivate sensibility, art and therapy and political action have to all be gathered.

In the sphere of precarious work, time has been fragmented and depersonalized. Social time is transformed into a sprawl of fractals, compatible fragments that can be recombined by the networked machine: this is why I speak of the fractalization of time.

Aesthetic perception—here properly conceived of as the realm of sensibility and aesthesia—is directly involved in the technological transformation of communication and work: in its attempt to efficiently interface with the connective environment, the conscious organism appears to increasingly inhibit what we call sensibility. By sensibility, I mean the faculty that enables human beings to interpret signs that are not verbal nor can be made so, the ability to understand what cannot be expressed in forms that have a finite syntax. This faculty reveals itself to be useless and even damaging in an integrated connective system, because sensibility tends to slow down the processes of interpretation, making them ambiguous and downgrading the competitive efficiency of the semiotic agent.

Sensibility is in time, and we need time to understand the hypercomplex communication of the body. Due to the acceleration of the info-rhythm, precarious workers are obliged to detect and interpret signs at an ever-accelerating pace, and their sensibility is disturbed. This is why therapy is increasingly involved in the political field of reactivating the social body and recomposing work in a process of subjectivation.

If we want to think through the relation between art and (schizo)therapy, we have to think in terms of the refrain. Guattari says that the refrain is a semiotic concatenation (*agencement*) that is able to latch onto the environment. Cosmic, terrestrial, social, and affective environments can be grasped and internalized thanks to refrains that we have in our minds, in our sensitive and sensible brains.

In his book *Chaosmosis*, Guattari speaks of the "aesthetic paradigm." This concept redefines the historical and social perspective, and it is fully integrated into the vision of ecosophy. An environmental consciousness adequate to the technological complexity of hypermodernity, ecosophy is based on the acknowledgment of the crucial role of aesthetics in the prospect of ecology.

Actually, aesthetics is the science dedicated to the study of the contact between the derma (the skin, the sensitive surface of our body-mind) and different chemical, physical, electromagnetic, electronic, and informational flows. Therefore, aesthetics has much to do with the modern psychopathology of contact, with the pathological effects of the acceleration of the info-flow and the precarization of social existence. Guattari views the universe as a continuum of diverse and interrelated entities in bodily contact with each other. It is both an organic and inorganic continuum, animal and machinic, mental and electronic, and the concatenation is made possible by *ritournelles*, semiotic markers of rhythm. Rhythm is the common substance of signs (word, music, vision) and the brain. The mind hooks onto the other (the other mind, nature, artificial, or social world) thanks to rhythmic concatenation.

In the past century, the century that trusted in the future, art was essentially involved in the business of acceleration. Futurism defined the relation between art, the social mind, and social life. The cult of energy marked the artistic zeitgeist, up to the saturation of collective perception and the paralysis of empathy. Futurist rhythm was the rhythm of info-acceleration, of violence and war.

Now we need refrains that disentangle singular existence from the social game of competition and productivity: refrains of psychic and sensitive autonomization, refrains of the singularization and sensibilization of breathing, once unchained from the congested pace of the immaterial assembly line of semio-capitalist production.

Once upon a time, pleasure was repressed by power. Now it is advertised and promised, and simultaneously postponed and deceived. This is the pornographic feature of semio-production in the sphere of the market.

The eye has taken the central place of human sensory life, but this ocular domination is a domination of merchandise, of promises that are never fulfilled and always postponed. In the current conditions of capitalist competition, acceleration is the trigger for panic, and panic is the premise to depression. Singularity is forgotten, erased, and cancelled in the erotic domain of semio-capitalism. The singularity of the voice and the singularity of words are subjected to the homogenization of exchange and valorization.

Social communication is submitted to techno-linguistic interfaces: in order to exchange meaning in the sphere of connectivity, conscious organisms have to adapt to the digital environment.

In order to accelerate the circulation of value, meaning is reduced to information, and techno-linguistic devices act as the communicative matrix. The matrix takes the place of the mother in the process of generating language.

But language and information do not overlap, and language cannot be resolved in exchangeability. In Ferdinand de Saussure's parlance, we may say that the infinity of the *parole* exceeds the recombinant logic of the *langue*, such that language can escape from the matrix and reinvent a social sphere of singular vibrations intermingling and projecting a new space for sharing, producing, and living.

Poetry opens the doors of perception to singularity.

Poetry is language's excess: poetry is what in language cannot be reduced to information, and is not exchangeable, but gives way to a new common ground of understanding, of shared meaning: the creation of a new world.

Poetry is a singular vibration of the voice. This vibration can create resonances, and resonances may produce common space, the place where:

lovers, who never
Could achieve fulfillment here, could show
Their bold lofty figures of heart-swings,
Their towers of ecstasy.

Vagrants

But tell me, who are these vagrants, these even a little
More transitory than we, these from the start
Violently wrung (and for whose sake?)
By a never-appeasable will? But it wrings them,
Bends them, slings them and swings them,
Throws them and catches them; as if from an oily,
More slippery air they come down
On the carpet worn thinner by their eternal leaping,
This carpet lost in the universe.
Stuck there like a plaster, as if the sky
Of the suburb had hurt the earth.
  —Rilke: "Fifth Elegy," verses 1–11

These verses can be read simultaneously as a metaphor for the condition of precarity, and as an annunciation of a place that we don't know, that we have never experienced: a place of the city, a square, a street, an apartment where suddenly lovers, who here (in the kingdom of valorization and exchange) never "could achieve fulfillment," toss their last ever-hoarded, ever hidden, unknown— to us—eternally valid coins of happiness.

There is no secret meaning in these words, but we can read in these verses a description of the frail architectures of collective happiness: "Their towers of ecstasy, their pyramid that long since, where there was no standing-ground were tremblingly propped together."

This place we don't know is the place we are looking for, in a social environment that has been impoverished by social precariousness, in a landscape that has been deserted. It is the place that will be able to warm the sensible sphere that has been deprived of the joy of singularity. It is the place of occupation, where movements are gathering: Tahrir square in Cairo, Plaza do Sol in Madrid, and Zuccotti Park in New York City.

We call poetry the semiotic concatenation that exceeds the sphere of exchange and the codified correspondence of the signifier and signified; it is the semiotic concatenation that creates new pathways of signification and opens the way to a reactivation of the relation between sensibility and time, as sensibility is the faculty that makes possible the singularity of the enunciation and the singularity of the understanding of a noncodified enunciation.

Viktor Shklovsky, the Russian formalist theorist, says that the specificity of literary language lies in the ability to treat words according to an unrepeatable singular procedure, that in Russian he calls *priem*: an artificial treatment of verbal matter generating effects of meaning never seen and codified before. Poetical procedure is a form of enstrangement (*ostranenie*, in Russian) that carries the word far and away from its common use.

"Art is not chaos," say Deleuze and Guattari in *What Is Philosophy?*, "but a composition of chaos that yields the vision or sensation, so that it constitutes, as Joyce says, a chaosmos" (Deleuze and Guattari 1994, 204–205). The relation between the organism and the environment is disturbed by the acceleration of info-stimula in the infosphere, by semiotic inflation, and by the saturation of attention and the conscious sensitive sphere of subjectivity. Art is recording and detecting this dissonance, as it simultaneously creates the aesthetic conditions for the perception and expression of new modes of becoming.

Relative to schizoanalysis, art is acting differently in two ways: it represents a diagnostic of the infospheric pollution of the psychosphere, but also a therapy treating the disturbed organism.

The refrain is the sensitive niche where we can create cosmos elaborating chaos.

Social movements can be described as a form of refrain: movements are the refrain of singularization, as they act to create spheres of singularity at the aesthetic and existential levels.

In the process of singularization that the movement makes possible, production, need, and consumption can be semiotized again, according to a new system of world expectations.

Changing the order of expectations is one of the main social transformations that a movement can produce: this change implies a cultural transformation but also a change in sensitivity, in the opening of the organism to the world and to the others.

Insurrection is a refrain helping to withdraw the psychic energies of society from the standardized rhythm of compulsory competition-consumerism, and helping to create an autonomous collective sphere. Poetry is the language of the movement as it tries to deploy a new refrain.

The Limits of the World

In the chapter of *Chaosmosis* that is dedicated to the aesthetic paradigm, Guattari speaks of the new modes of the submission and standardization of subjectivity produced by network technologies and by neoliberal globalization. Simultaneously, he tries to find new pathways to autonomous subjectivation.

As far as concerns the first side of the problem, he writes:

> Subjectivity is standardized through a communication which evacuates as much as possible trans-semiotic and amodal enunciative compositions. Thus it slips towards the progressive

effacement of polysemy, prosody, gesture, mimicry and posture, to the profit of a language rigorously subjected to scriptural machines and their mass media avatars. In its extreme contemporary forms it amounts to an exchange of information tokens calculable as bits and reproducible on computers.

In this type of deterritorialised assemblage, the capitalist Signifier, a simulacrum of the imaginary of power, has the job of overcoding all the other Universes of value. (Guattari 1995, 104–5)

Digital technology is canceling the singular enunciative composition of polysemy, gesture, and voice, and tends to produce a language that is subjected to the linguistic machinery. While analyzing the standardization of language, Guattari simultaneously looks for a line of escape from the informational submission (*assujettissement*).

An initial chaosmic folding consists in making the powers of chaos co-exist with those of the highest complexity. It is by a continuous coming-and-going at an infinite speed that the multiplicities of entities differentiate into ontologically heterogeneous complexions and become chaotised in abolishing their figural diversity and by homogenising themselves within the same being-non-being. In a way, they never stop diving into an umbilical chaotic zone where they lose their extrinsic references and coordinates, but from where they re-emerge invested with new charges of complexity. It is during this chaosmic folding that an interface is installed—an interface between the sensible finitude of existential Territories and the trans-sensible infinitude of the Universe of reference bound to them. Thus one oscillates, on the one hand, between a finite world of reduced speed, where limits always loom up behind limits, constraints behind constraints, systems of coordinates behind other systems of coordinates, without ever arriving at the ultimate tangent of a being-matter which recedes everywhere and, on the other hand, Universes of infinite speed where being can't be denied anymore, where it gives itself in its intrinsic differences, in its heterogeneous qualities. The machine, every species of machine, is always at the junction of the finite and infinite, at this point of negotiation between complexity and chaos. (Guattari 1995, 110–111)

Guattari here questions the relation between the finite and infinite in the sphere of language. He is mapping the territory of the informational rhizome, that was not yet completely discovered when *Chaosmosis* was written. The ambiguity of the info-rhizomatic territory is crystal clear: info-technology is standardizing subjectivity and language, inscribing techno-linguistic interfaces which automatize enunciation.

We are tracing here the dynamic of a disaster, the disaster that capitalism is inserting into hyper-modern subjectivity, the disaster of acceleration and panic. But simultaneously we have to look for a rhythm which may open a further landscape, a landscape beyond panic and beyond the precarious affects of loneliness and despair.

In the chapter on aesthetic paradigm in *Chaosmosis*, Guattari rethinks the question of singularity in terms of sensitive finitude and the possible infinity of language.

The conscious and sensitive organism, the living individuality walking towards extinction, is finite. But the creation of possible universes of meaning is infinite. Desire is the field of this tendency of the finite towards a becoming-infinite.

> To produce new infinities from a submersion in sensible finitude, infinities not only charged with virtuality but with potentialities actualisable in given situations, circumventing or dissociating oneself from the Universals itemised by traditional arts, philosophy, and psychoanalysis [...] a new love of the unknown... (Guattari 1995, 161)

The finitude of the conscious and sensitive organism is the place where we imagine projections of infinity which are not only virtual, but also a potentiality of life, and that can be actualized in situations.

We are on the threshold of a deterritorialized and rhizomatic world, realizing the antioedipal, schizoform dream. But this dream is becoming true in the form of a global nightmare of financial derealization. On this threshold we have to imagine a politics and an ethics of singularity, breaking our ties with expectations of infinite growth, infinte consumption, and infinite expansion of the self.

In the preface to his *Tractatus Logico-Philosophicus*, Wittgenstein writes: "in order to draw a limit to thinking we should have to be able to think both sides of this limit (we should therefore have to be able to think what cannot be thought)." (Wittgenstein 1922, 27)

And he also writes:

> The limits of my language mean the limits of my world. Logic pervades the world: the limits of the world are also its limits. So we cannot say in logic, "The world has this in it, and this, but not that." For that would appear to presuppose that we were excluding certain possibilities, and this cannot be the case, since it would require that logic should go beyond the limits of the world; for only in that way could it view those limits from the other side as well. We cannot think

what we cannot think; so what we cannot think
we cannot say either. (Wittgenstein 1922, 68)

And finally, he writes: "The subject does not belong
to the world: rather, it is a limit of the world."

When Wittgenstein says that the limits of language are the limits of the world, he is saying
something that should be read in two different
ways. First, he is saying: what we cannot say we
cannot do, we cannot experience, we cannot live,
because only in the sphere of language can we
interact with the reality of Being. But he is also
saying that, because the world is what resides
within the limits of our language, what therefore
lies beyond the limits of language will only be able
to be lived and experienced once our language is
able to elaborate that sphere of Being that lies
beyond the present limit.

In fact, the philosopher writes: "the subject
does not belong to the world, rather it is a limit
of the world."

The potency and extension of language
depends on the consistency of the subject, on his
or her vision, on his or her situation. And the
extension of my world depends on the potency
of my language.

Guattari calls "chaosmosis" the process of going
beyond the limits of the world, and he calls this
going beyond resemiotization: i.e., a redefinition

of the semiotic limit, which is also the limit of the experimentability of the world.

Scientists call this effect of autopoietic morphogenesis "emergence": a new form emerges and takes shape when logical linguistic conditions make it possible to see it and to name it. Let's try to understand our present situation from this point of view.

Digital financial capitalism has created a closed reality which cannot be overcome with the techniques of politics, of conscious organized voluntary action, and of government.

Only an act of language can give us the ability to see and to create a new human condition, where we now only see barbarianism and violence.

Only an act of language escaping the technical automatisms of financial capitalism will make possible the emergence of a new life form. The new form of life will be the social and instinctual body of the general intellect, the social and instinctual body that the general intellect is deprived of inside the present conditions of financial dictatorship.

Only the reactivation of the body of the general intellect—the organic, existential, historical finitude that embodies the potency of the general intellect—will be able to imagine new infinities.

In the intersection of the finite and infinite, in the point of negotiation between complexity and chaos, it will be possible to generate a degree of complexity greater than the degree of complexity that financial capitalism is able to manage and elaborate.

Language has an infinite potency, but the exercise of language happens in finite conditions of history and existence. Thanks to the establishment of a limit, the world comes into existence as a world of language. Grammar, logic, and ethics are based on the institution of a limit. But infinity remains unmeasurable.

Poetry is the reopening of the indefinite, the ironic act of exceeding the established meaning of words.

In every sphere of human action, grammar is the establishment of limits defining a space of communication. Today the economy is the universal grammar traversing the different levels of human activity. Language is defined and limited by its economic exchangeability: this effects a reduction of language to information, an incorporation of techno-linguistic automatisms into the social circulation of language.

Nevertheless, while social communication is a limited process, language is boundless: its potentiality is not limited to the limits of the signified. Poetry is language's excess, the signifier disentangled from the limits of the signified.

Irony, the ethical form of the excessive power of language, is the infinite game that words play to create and to skip and to shuffle meaning.

A social movement, at the end of the day, should use irony as semiotic insolvency, as a mechanism of disentangling language, behavior, and action from the limits of the symbolic debt.

IRONY AND CYNICISM

Mass *Zynismus*

In his book *The Courage of Truth*, a transcription of lectures delivered at the College de France in 1984, Michel Foucault speaks of Diogenes and the other ancient philosophers known as cynics, and defines their thought as a practice of telling the truth (*parrhesia*). Twenty-five years later, the word cynicism has acquired a totally different meaning, almost the opposite: the cynic is someone who routinely lies to everyone, especially to him or herself. An intimate lie, the contradiction between speech and belief, lies at the core of contemporary cynicism. Still, there remains a kind of consistency between the ancient notion of cynicism—rigorous truthfulness, individualism, ascetic behavior, and disdain for power—and our own, which consists largely of lip service, moral unreliability, and conformist subjugation to those in power. This consistency lies in an awareness of the ambiguous nature of language, and an ability to suspend the relation between language and reality, particularly in the ethical sphere. Cynicism, therefore, is closely related to irony. Both are rhetorical forms and ethical stances that require the suspension of the relation between reality and language. Some German philosophers, like Paul Tillich and Peter Sloterdijk, use two different words to distinguish the ancient Greek cynicism discussed by Foucault and our own: *kynismus* and *zynismus*.

Modern *zynismus* can be understood by recalling Stanley Kubrick's 1999 film, *Eyes Wide Shut*, an artistic gravestone to the modern illusion of progressive Enlightenment. Bill and Alice, a happily married couple (Fridolin and Albertine in Arthur Schnitzler's novel *Dream Story* [1926], which inspired Kubrick's screenplay) are expressions of an awareness that truth can never be spoken because the social game is based on the power of lies. If you don't accept the language of deceit, no one will listen to you. This is where Kubrick's survey of the twentieth century arrives. It began with Dax: the upright colonel played by Kirk Douglas, who fights the cowardice of military power in *Paths of Glory* (1957). Dax believes in ethical righteousness. He has the strength and courage to oppose evil because he thinks that evil can be stopped and defeated.

Bill Harford (played by Tom Cruise) in *Eyes Wide Shut* is still able to recognize misdeeds and distinguish right from wrong, but he knows that nothing can be done to stop and defeat evil. Despite moral unhappiness, he must bend to evil if he wants to survive.

At the end of a century that believed in the future, *zynismus* seems to be the only accepted language, the only cool behavior. "Cool" is a keyword in contemporary cynicism. Andre Glucksmann, in his 1981 book *Cynicism and Passion*, suggests that the only alternative to cynicism is passion, but that's wrong.

The real alternative to cynicism is not passion, but irony.

In *Critique of Cynical Reason*, Peter Sloterdijk argues that cynicism is the prevailing mindset throughout the post-'68 era. To Sloterdijk, cynicism doesn't denote an exceptional social character: it is the typical state of mind. As he describes the ancient notion of cynicism, "It violates normal usage to describe cynicism as a universal and diffuse phenomenon; as it is commonly conceived, cynicism is not diffuse but striking, not universal but peripheral and highly individual." (Sloterdijk 1988, 4) And this is the most important difference between *kynismus* and *zynismus*: while Diogenes and his fellow kynicists were ascetic individualists rejecting the acquiescence to the law of the powerful, the modern zynicists are the conformist majority, fully aware that the law of the powerful is bad, but bending to it because there's nothing else to do. Unlike the ancient cynism, modern *zynismus* is not disruptive. It is an internalization of the impotence of truth. As Sloterdijk writes:

> … [T]his is the essential point in modern cynicism, the ability of its bearers to work, in spite of anything that might happen, and especially, after anything that might happen … cynics are not dumb, and every now and then they certainly see the nothingness to which everything leads. Their psychic (*seelish*) apparatus has become elastic enough to incorporate as a survival factor a permanent doubt about their own activities. They know what they are doing, but they do it because, in the short run, the force of circumstances and the instinct for self-preservation are speaking the same language; and they are telling them that it has to be so. (Sloterdijk 1988, 5)

Contemporary mass cynicism can be linked to two different sources: the failure of twentieth-century utopian ideologies, and the perception that the exploitation of labor, competition, and war are inevitable and irreversible. Mass cynicism results from the dissolution of social solidarity. Globalization and the systemic precariousness of the labor market resulting from neoliberal deregulation have imposed competition as the inescapable, generalized mode of relation among social actors. Workers, once linked by a sense of social solidarity and common political hope, are now forced to think in cynical terms: survival of the fittest.

Within the '68 movement, different cultures and political tendencies coexisted. Some dreamed of the historical *Aufhebung*: the institution of a proletarian dictatorship, who would seize power in their own hands. Like Hegelians, the doctrinaire Marxists dreamed of a triumph of reason in which the good guys were destined to win. To remain with the proletariat was to be on the winning side of history. When the wind turned and the workers' movement was defeated, neoliberalism provided an ideology for a new wave of capitalist aggressivity. Those who wished to remain on the winning side of history decided to stay with the winners because all that is real is rational, in the end! In their dialectical scheme, whoever wins is right, and whoever is right is destined to win.

The majority '68-era activists were not orthodox dialecticians and did not expect any *Aufhebung*. We never believed in the end of historical complexity and the final establishment of the perfect form of communism. This sounded false to students and young workers, who were seeking autonomy in the present, not communism in the future.

Today's neoliberal conformists are the perverted heirs of '68. Those who came to power after '89 in Russia, the US, and Europe are not as free from ideology as they pretend. Their ideology is a dogmatic faith in the unquestionability of the economy. The economy has taken the place of the all-encompassing Hegelian Dialectic of Reason. Bending to the dominant power, neoliberals accept (economic) necessity. The only difficulty is that no one knows which trends will achieve dominance in the complicated becoming of future events. Consequently, cynicism—despite its apparent inevitability—is weak, as a position. No one knows what will happen next. Unpredictable events cannot be reduced to logical necessity.

Irony and *Zynismus*

Sloterdijk is not alone in his conflation of mass cynicism and irony. As he writes in *Critique*: "From the very bottom, from the declassed urban intelligentsia, and from the very top, from the summits of statesmanly consciousness, signals penetrate serious thinking, signals that provide evidence of a radical, ironic treatment (*Ironizierung*) of ethics and of social conventions, as if universal laws existed only for the stupid, while the fatally clever smile plays on the lips of those in the know." (Sloterdijk 1988, 4)

Of course irony—like sarcasm, its more aggressive form—can be an expression of cynicism. But irony and cynicism should not be conflated. Irony can be a linguistic tool for rationalizing cynical behavior. Both irony and cynicism imply a dissociation of language and behavior from consciousness: what you say is not what you think. But this dissociation takes different turns in irony and cynicism.

Vladimir Jankélévitch defines cynicism in the following way in his book *Irony*: "[C]ynicism is often deceived moralism, and an extreme form of irony ..." (Jankélévitch 1936, 23) Cynicism, he implies, is a learned form of irony, used for the pleasure of shocking the philistines.

Cynicism is the philosophy of exaggeration (*surenchère*): as Jankélévitch writes, "irony after Socrates tends to be exaggeration of moral radicalism ..." Cynicism is deceived moralism, a judgment of behavior that depends on a fixed system of (moral) values. Dialectical materialism, the philosophy of the past century, implied a form of moralism: anything (progress, socialism, etc.) that moves in the direction of history is *good*, whatever opposes the movement of history is *bad*. Post-'68 cynicism results from a painful awakening. Since the truth has not been fulfilled, we'll align ourselves with the untruth. And this is where irony and cynicism differ. Ironic discourse never presupposes the existence of a truth that will be fulfilled or realized. Irony implies the infinite process of interpretation, whereas cynicism results from a (lost) faith. The cynic has lost his or her faith; the ironist never had a faith to begin. In Jankélévitch's words: "[I]rony is never disenchanted for the good reason that irony has refused to be enchanted." (Jankélévitch 1936, 24)

And yet, irony and cynicism both start with a suspension of disbelief in both the moral content of truth, and morality's true content. Both cynics and ironists understand that the True and the Good do not exist in God's mind or in History, and that human behavior isn't based upon respect for any law. In *Masochism: Coldness and Cruelty*, Deleuze says this of irony and the law: "Irony is still in the process or movement which bypasses the law as a merely secondary power and aims at transcending it toward a higher principle." (Deleuze 1989, 86)

Neither irony nor cynicism believe in the true foundation of law. But the cynical person bends to the law while mocking its false and pretentious values, while the ironic person escapes the law altogether, creating a linguistic space where law has no effectiveness. The cynic wants to be on the side of power, even though he doesn't believe in its righteousness. The ironist simply refuses the game, recreating the world on the basis of language that is incongruent with reality. Whereas mass cynicism (*zynismus*) has to do with aggression, both suffered and inflicted, irony is based upon sympathy. While cynical behavior pivots upon a false relation with interlocutors, irony involves a shared suspension of reality. The use of irony implies a shared sense of assumptions and implications between oneself and one's listeners. Irony cannot be conflated with lying. As Jankélévitch writes:

> Lying is a state of war, and irony is a state of peace. The liar is not in agreement with the cheated. The gullible consciousness is late in relation with the lying consciousness, which is trying to maintain its advantage. Irony, instead, is crediting the interlocutor of sagacity and treats him/her as a true partner of true dialogue. Irony incites intellection, and is calling a fraternal echo of understanding. (Jankélévitch 1936, 24)

The conflation between power and the incessant movement of historical events toward the good that defined Marxist thought was sundered. Here the fork between irony and cynicism opens.

Irony suspends the semantic value of the signifier to freely choose among a thousand possible interpretations. Ironic interpretations of events presuppose a common understanding between speakers and listeners; a sympathy among those who, engaged in the ironic act, arrive at a common autonomy from the dictatorship of the signified.

Sleep

In the '70s, while reading Deleuze and Guattari, the consciousness of the autonomous movement discovered that reality has no meaning: the meaning of reality has to be created by the movement itself. So the autonomous movement broke free of the idea that the ethical horizon is marked by historical necessity, and opened its mind to the ironic mood, which means singularization of ethical responsibility and political choice. In this (postdialectical) space of moral indetermination, both linguistic enunciation and political action are devoid of any ontological foundation.

The will of power and research of the good, which were linked in the framework of historical ideology, are now diverging. Here the fork of irony and cynicism opens.

Irony suspends the semantic value of the signifier and chooses freely among a thousand possible interpretations. The ironic interpretation implies and presupposes a common ground of understanding among the interlocutors, a sympathy among those who are involved in the ironic act, and a common autonomy from the dictatorship of the signified.

Cynicism starts from the same suspension, but is a slavish modulation of irony: irony at the service of power. While irony does not postulate the existence of any reality, cynicism postulates the inescapable reality of power, particularly the power of the economy.

Irony is an opening of a game of infinite possibilities; cynicism is a dissociation of ethics and possibility. The cynical mood starts from the idea that ethical action has no possibility of succeeding.

The ironist sleeps happily because nothing can awake her from her dreams. The cynicist sleeps a light sleep, he dreams nightmares, and he gets up as soon as power calls him.

References

Agamben, Giorgio. 2006. *Language and Death: The Place of Negativity*. Trans. Karen Pinkus and Michael Hardt. Minneapolis: University of Minnesota Press.

Baudrillard, Jean. 1975. *The Mirror of Production*. Trans. Mark Poster. New York: The Telos Press, Ltd.

———. 1993. *Symbolic Exchange and Death*. Trans. Iain Hamilton Grant. London: Sage Publications.

———. 1996. "Global Debt and Parallel Universe." Trans. Francois Debrix. www.ctheory.net/articles.aspx?id=164.

Benasayag, Miguel and Gérard Schmidt. 2003. *Les passions tristes: Souffrance psychique et crise sociale*. Trans. Line Kozlowski. Paris: Editions la Découverte.

Benda, Julien. 1993. *Discours à la nation européenne*. Paris: Galimard.

Campagna, Federico. 2011. "Recurring Dreams—The Red Heart of Fascism." *Through Europe*. http://th-rough.eu/writers/campagna-eng/recurring-dreams-red-heart-fascism

Deleuze, Gilles and Félix Guattari. 1977. *Anti-Oedipus: Capitalism and Schizophrenia*. Trans. Robert Hurley, Mark Seem and Helen R. Lane. New York: Viking Press.

———. 1987. *A Thousand Plateaus: Capitalism and Schizophrenia*. Trans. Brian Massumi. Minneapolis: University of Minnesota Press.

——. 1994. *What Is Philosophy?* Trans. Hugh Tomlinson and Graham Burchell. New York: Columbia University Press.

Deleuze, Gilles and Leopold von Sacher-Masoch. 1989. *Masochism: Coldness and Cruelty & Venus in Furs*. Trans. Jean McNeil. New York: Zone Books.

Derrida, Jacques. 1980. *Writing and Difference*. Trans. Alan Bass. Chicago: University of Chicago Press.

Flaubert, Gustave. 1990. *Préface à la vie d'écrivain*. Ed. Geneviève Bollème. Paris: Éditions du Seuil.

Foucault, Michel. 2008. *The Birth of Biopolitics: Lectures at the Collège de France, 1978–1979*. Ed. Michel Senellart. Trans. Graham Burchell. New York: Palgrave Macmillan.

Foucault, Michel. 2011. *The Courage of Truth (The Government of Self and Others II): Lectures at the Collège de France, 1983–1984*. Ed. Frédéric Gros. Trans. Graham Burchell. New York: Palgrave Macmillan.

Glucksmann, André. 1981. *Cynisme et passion*. Paris: Grasset.

Goldsen, Rose Kohn. 1977. *The Show and Tell Machine: How Television Works and Works You Over*. New York: The Dial Press.

Goodman, Steve. 2010. *Sonic Warfare: Sound, Affect, and the Ecology of Fear*. Cambridge: The MIT Press.

Graeber, David. 2011. *Debt: The First 5,000 Years*. New York: Melville House.

Greimas, Algirdas Julien. 1970. *Du sens: Essais sémiotiques, tome 1*. Paris: Éditions du Seuil.

Guattari, Félix. 1995. *Chaosmosis: An Ethico-Aesthetic Paradigm*. Trans. P. Bains and J. Pefanis. Bloomington: Indiana University Press.

——. 2011. *The Machinic Unconscious: Essays in Schizoanalysis*. Trans. Taylor Adkins. Los Angeles: Semiotext(e).

Jankélévitch, Vladimir. 1964. *L'ironie*. Paris: Flammarion.

Kaplan, Frédéric. 2011. "Quand les mots valent de l'or." *Le Monde diplomatique* November 2011: 28.

Kroker, Arthur and Michael A. Weinstein. 1994. *Data Trash: The Theory of the Virtual Class*. New York: St. Martin's Press.

Lazzarato, Maurizio. 2012. *The Making of the Indebted Man*. Trans. Joshua David Jordan. Los Angeles: Semiotext(e).

Marinetti, Filippo Tommaso. 2006. *Critical Writings, new edition*. Ed. Günter Berghaus. Trans. Doug Thompson. New York: Farrar, Straus and Giroux.

Meadows, Donella H., Dennis L. Meadows, Jørgen Randers, and William W. Behrens III. 1972. *The Limits to Growth*. New York: Universe Books.

Muraro, Luisa. 1994. *L'ordine simbolico della madre*. Rome: Editori Riuniti.

Recalcati, Massimo. 2010. *L'uomo senza inconscio: Figure della nuova clinica psicoanalitica*. Milan: Cortina Raffaello.

Sardello, Robert J. and Randolph Severson. 1983. *Money and the Soul of the World*. Dallas: The Pegasus Foundation.

Seabrook, John. 1994. "E-mail to Bill." *The New Yorker* 69 (45): 52.

Shell, Marc. 1982. *Money, Language, and Thought: Literary and Philosophical Economies from the Medieval to the Modern Era*. Berkeley: The University of California Press.

Sloterdijk, Peter. 1988. *Critique of Cynical Reason*. Trans. Michael Eldred. Minneapolis: University of Minnesota Press.

Spinrad, Norman. 1969. *Bug Jack Barron*. New York: Walker & Company.

Wiener, Norbert. 1961. *Cybernetics, or the Control and Communication in the Animal and the Machine, 2nd edition*. Cambridge: The MIT Press.

Wittgenstein, Ludwig. 1922. *Tractatus Logico-Philosophicus*. Trans. C. K. Ogden. London: Routledge and Kegan Paul.

semiotext(e) intervention series

———————————————————